# ENHANCING YOUR CREATIVE POTENTIAL

*By*
ROB CUBBON

*RobCubbon.com*

Enhance Your Creative Potential
**Rob Cubbon**

Published by Rob Cubbon Ltd. *http://robcubbon.com*

© 2023 Rob Cubbon

No portion of this publication may be reproduced or transmitted in any form or by any means, electronic or mechanical, including, but not limited to, audio recordings, facsimiles, photocopying, or information storage and retrieval systems without explicit written permission from the author or publisher.

old passions, and make meaningful contributions to the world.

It is an invitation to embrace the limitless possibilities of creativity and harness its profound impact on your life. It's never too late to unleash your creative potential.

## Why am I writing this book?

I don't fit nicely into society's stereotype. And it's my guess you don't either. The stereotype came from many decades ago. Times may have changed, but attitudes take longer to change. This book is about changing along with the times rather than being left behind.

I'm in my fifties, divorced, childless, single, and happy. I spend my time as creatively as possible. It's of huge benefit to me. I have written eight books and numerous blog posts and articles. I've created thousands of t-shirt designs, book cover designs, stories, songs, etc. I like creating things and putting them out there. I'm so lucky I can spend my time doing this.

However, I used to live a rather humdrum existence. In my 20s and 30s, I spent most of my time commuting to work on London's underground railway to spend 8 hours in a drab office sitting in front of a computer. I was too exhausted in the evenings to do anything other than watch TV. I could have gone to "open mics" and performed on the guitar, but I never felt able. I was disheartened by the prospect of traveling again after the daily commute and the competition was huge.

# Introduction

We are experiencing an era of unparalleled uncertainty. We're coming out of the pandemic with economic problems, toxic polarization, rising geopolitical tensions, and the peril of climate change hanging over us. Creativity is needed to solve these tough problems.

By nurturing creativity, we gain the capacity to think beyond traditional boundaries and use our imagination to address complex problems.

Beyond just generating ideas, creativity also enhances empathy and increases connections. It helps us better understand different viewpoints and build bridges of understanding, even when society seems increasingly divided.

While offering immense opportunities, technologies such as Artificial Intelligence (AI) also brings uncertainty. Automation poses risks to job security, potentially increasing unemployment and exacerbating income inequality. Moreover, the rapid rate of technological change makes us feel overwhelmed and unprepared to adjust.

This book explores the transformative power of creativity and aims to inspire and guide you on a journey of self-discovery, reinvention, and artistic expression. By unlocking your creative potential, you can experience a profound sense of fulfillment, reignite

So, inevitably, I did nothing in the evenings and the weekends other than relax and prepare for the working week. I had no time for creativity. My guitar sat in the corner of the room, gathering dust. I spent little of my time on artistic endeavors and I thought I'd written my last song when I was in my early 20s. Well, that's sad, I thought. I guess being an adult means you can't do fun things anymore.

Now I live in a different city. Chiang Mai in Thailand isn't nearly as big as London, but it is a place that fosters creativity. Even a small city like Chiang Mai has many music venues. If I wanted to, I could play with other musicians every evening of the week. And, as part of my business, I regularly do t-shirt designs, book cover designs, write articles and blogs, and create videos for YouTube. I have a compulsion to create things and publish them.

Let me tell you more about my creative output. Not only do I enjoy these creative activities, they also involve engaging with other people. This is my bliss.

## Music

I often play music with other musicians. Making music with other people is special. These musicians elevate me to a higher level. Sometimes, a musician's talent is such that they lift everyone around them.

Talking of becoming a better musician. I remember when I was in my teens, I was very serious about playing guitar and being in a band with a few friends. We had the usual teenage dreams of going on the road and becoming famous rock stars. Our little group disbanded when the stresses of job hunting and adult life started. However, I remember thinking later that I was a decent guitarist at that time and I used to lament that my guitar playing skills had regressed since then. And I assumed I would never again be as good as I was in my teenage years. However, I'm definitely a better guitarist and musician now. I understand more about music. My knowledge of chords, scales, the box system of guitar soloing, and of song structure is better. My technique is better. My knowledge of guitar care is better. I know how to get a better sound out of my instrument.

Added to this, I'm a better singer now. I find that difficult to believe, especially as I've abused my throat and lungs by smoking cigarettes and other substances in some of the intervening years. I was never the lead singer in the little bands I was in in my teenage years. But now, I force myself to "open mics" in Chiang Mai, where I have to get on stage and sing while accompanying myself. And I've improved because of recent experiences. Also, I now sing harmonies with other singers. I never knew I could do that. My improvement in music in my mid-50s delights me.

I used to write songs. Lots of songs. I wrote so many songs that I can't remember half of them. I wrote my first song at 8 or 9 years of age. It had two chords and consisted of a four line verse repeated over and over. And so I continued. I wrote stupid little love songs in my adolescence when I was a lifetime away from falling in love. And, in my teenage years, I wrote songs for the bands I played in. But then, sadly, I stopped. I'd started working. The exertion of employment and commuting knocked the creativity out of me. So, I gave up. I remember the last song I wrote in the early 90s. Or half wrote. It was just a series of verses with no satisfying chorus. An unfinished work. I regretted that this was something I once did and loved doing, but no longer do. I just assumed it was all part of growing up: you're young, you have fun creating things, then you grow up, and you stop having fun.

Now I realize this isn't the way it has to be. Making music has increased my creativity in other ways. Old neural pathways of thoughts, feelings, and emotions have reopened in my mind. Now, after a 30 year hiatus, I'm writing songs again. This has made me so happy. I can now do something I had thought I was unable to do for over three decades. Thirty years is a long time to cut yourself off from something special to you. And, just recently, I finally wrote a satisfying chorus to the song I thought was the last song I ever wrote in the early 90s.

Music is definitely my first and greatest passion. But music isn't my only creative outlet.

# Writing

When I was a kid, I also used to write stupid little short stories. Dumb little spy thrillers that were similar to James Bond movies. Daring do's of handsome alpha males in 1980s London. The thought of it bores me now, but it interested me then. My love of writing was then revived decades later when the Internet started to get interesting. In 2005, I started blogging at [RobCubbon.com](RobCubbon.com). I started writing about what I knew. And, in 2005, that was primarily print design and desktop publishing. Blogging and social media were in their infancy in those days, and I managed to get a tiny following and traffic from Google. I quickly developed a writing style and then branched out into writing non-fiction books. The first was published in 2012. Since then, I've written eight books. This book is my ninth.

I also journal. I was encouraged to start during the pandemic. I didn't "get it" at first. But I do now. Journaling lets you get random thoughts off your head onto paper, or onto Google Drive's servers, in my case. I usually write 500 words a day. It is over 200,000 words now. That's as much as a 500 page novel.

# Artwork

My other creative outlet is art. Kinda. Ever since the early 90s, when I was working night shifts in newspapers, I have enjoyed playing with Photoshop and other graphics applications. I was always interested in art. But my slapdash and gauche nature meant I would sometimes make a mess, spill paints, or make the paper dirty with my hands. I remember thinking that Photoshop could change society. I got the first inclination of how technology can "alter reality" by cloning out imperfections on a face, for example. Now, we take all this for granted. And new technologies associated with Artificial Intelligence (AI) make Photoshop look like a kid's color-by-numbers book (more of that later).

But fakery aside, the most marvelous thing about Photoshop, for me, was Command-Z. Now it didn't matter if I made a mistake. Now, if I accidentally deleted something, I could undo, and not have to start again. I familiarized myself with all of Photoshop's capabilities during those long night shifts. These skills benefited me as I subsequently set up a graphic and web design business, getting new clients through Google traffic from the blog.

I still love messing around with Photoshop and other graphics tools. I love enhancing my own photography—creating eye-catching graphics, choosing fonts, colors, and broadcasting images and videos into the world through the Internet.

Photoshop changed the world. It actually added a new word to the English dictionary. And so did Google. Era defining technologies.

Which brings me onto my next point, Artificial Intelligence.

## Artificial intelligence

Around about 1450, Johannes Gutenberg introduced the metal movable-type printing press in Europe. This invention set off a chain of events that meant ordinary people could interpret the Bible without priests and holy men interpreting it for them. And, later, it meant a greater proliferation of books and pamphlets disseminating more information than was previously available. The printing press was intrinsically linked to the Reformation, the Renaissance, the scientific revolution, and other movements in Europe that shaped that period. It ultimately meant that a greater number of people could become writers and communicate with an increasingly literate society. To a certain extent, it democratized communication. It wasn't just the elite who could publish.

I feel lucky (if that's the right word) to have lived through two similar technological breakthroughs in media and society. The first I experienced was through Photoshop, desktop publishing, the Internet, and Web 2.0. I was extremely optimistic about these technologies. Like Gutenberg's movable type, it allowed for a great democratization of communication. I didn't care for social media, the rise of online hate, and cat photos. But all technologies are used for good, bad, and banal. One of the most successful books to be printed on the first European printing presses was about how to correctly identify a witch.

Which brings me to Artificial Intelligence. I have been using both ChatGPT, a large language model (LLM) chatbot, other LLMs, and various AI image generators recently, and they have greatly enhanced my creativity.

I'm using an AI chatbot to write this book. Before you throw this book in the trash in disgust, please be assured that these words are my own. I'm writing this book on an iPad in a crowded cafe right now. But the book's plan, the ideas, and the examples within these pages were greatly enhanced by ChatGPT, and I'm not afraid to admit it.

There are many parts to writing a book. The first is planning out the chapters or the skeleton plan of the book. You then do the research. Later comes the actual writing. I find writing quite easy. I just sit at an iPad and touch type. The ideas flow from my brain, through my fingers, to Google's servers, and then on to, hopefully, someone else's brain. The hard part is knowing what to write next. This is where ChatGPT comes in. It's an ideas machine. It will suggest avenues of inquiry you might not have thought about. It's like a helpful co-writer sitting next to you, saying, "what about this?"

I also create a lot of images and graphics for my business. I sell a lot of books on Amazon, not just non-fiction books like this one but planners, activity books, coloring books, etc. These all need attractive covers and illustrations. This is another avenue for my creativity. I now use AI image generators like Midjourney to create the imagery and graphics that go in the books. Prompting an image generator and then messing around with the resulting image in Photoshop is more creative fun. And fun that has been enhanced by technology.

What evils will come from Artificial Intelligence? I don't know. I'm sure Gutenberg didn't guess his invention would be used to identify witches. I'm sure the pioneers of the early Internet didn't envisage online hate, misinformation, and cat videos. But, I know that creativity is more often a force for good than bad. People across the world are suffering. Creativity heals.

## What to expect from this book

Now you know a little about me, let's talk about you.

This book is designed to make you happier. Creativity has numerous health benefits and will help you in your professional and personal life. In the next chapter, I explain how creativity benefits you and how a lack of creativity has pushed people into a hopeless rut. Creativity is fun and fun isn't just for children.

There are a number of factors that are blocking your creativity. I will tell you how to unblock the blocks, rekindle old hobbies, ignite new inspiration, and enjoy uplifting activities with a new group of friends, all similarly inspired by the gift of creativity. Creativity is rarely a lonely practice.

I then will give you a few suggestions of how you can prioritize your passions, use creativity both for business and pleasure, and set the groundwork for creativity. We'll find the creative bliss you wish to follow and see how we can make time in your schedule for it. I then list a variety of creative practices and pastimes you can engage with today. This book is practical as well as theoretical.

Finally, I will leave you with chapters about technology, maintaining a creative lifestyle, creativity in the workplace, and sharing the fruits of your passions.

And, I have interspersed all the chapters with stories from the present and the past about how individuals have used their creativity in helpful and inspiring ways.

Let's start with Frida Kahlo.

# Frida Kahlo

Frida Kahlo was born in 1907 in Coyoacán, Mexico. At the age of 18, Kahlo was involved in a devastating bus accident that left her with a broken spinal column, a broken pelvis, and multiple fractures. The accident had a profound impact on her and caused her lifelong pain. It was during her recovery, confined to her bed, that Kahlo discovered her passion for painting.

Using a mirror placed above her bed, Kahlo began to create self-portraits that became a recurring theme in her art. She sought to embody her physical pain as well as her identity as a woman of Mexican and Indigenous heritage.

In addition to her physical ailments, Kahlo also faced emotional challenges, including a tumultuous marriage to the renowned Mexican artist Diego Rivera.

Art, therefore, became a sanctuary for Kahlo, a place where she could channel her pain. Through her art, she found a sense of control in a world that often felt overwhelming.

Kahlo's work gained recognition for its raw authenticity. She became a prominent figure in the art world, paving the way for female artists for generations to come. Her paintings, such as "The Two Fridas" and "Self-Portrait with Thorn Necklace and Hummingbird," continue to resonate with audiences worldwide.

Frida Kahlo's love for art became her sanctuary,

providing an avenue for self-expression, healing, and resilience. Her ability to transform her pain into art not only contributed to her own personal growth but also left an indelible mark on the world, inspiring countless other individuals to find strength and beauty in their own struggles.

# The importance of enhancing your creativity

Why do I consider creativity so important to your mental, physical, spiritual, and social well-being?

In our early years, our lives are characterized by peaks and troughs. Then there is a "leveling" out period as we enter the next stages of our lives. Different people flourish in different periods. All the way through, we have to juggle our commitments to ensure a healthy work-life balance. Life's pressures, as well as societal expectations, weigh heavily.

Men can often mask feelings of self-doubt behind a façade of bravado and machismo. They often find themselves with few support networks and lack examples of other men creatively navigating challenges.

Similarly, women have historically been hindered in their creative pursuits due to societal norms and gender biases. They've been discouraged from artistic endeavors, ignored in creative circles, and denied equal opportunities. Even now, women continue to face hurdles in certain creative domains, including inadequate representation and unequal pay.

Technologies such as AI and automation are becoming increasingly prevalent and are impacting certain job sectors. The old certainties of the job for life and the breadwinner are being eroded. For some, there is, quite simply, no Plan B.

This book is a Plan B. Or, should we call it Plan C for Creativity? I'm going to show you that creativity is not just for the talented, the lucky, or the rich. I will share how unleashing creativity is the answer to a lack of direction, energy, intimacy, and spirituality.

But first, what are the benefits of releasing creativity?

# It's fun!

Engaging in creative activities will allow us to express ourselves in a society where some feel they don't have a voice. It provides a sense of personal fulfillment as we tap into our passions, leading to a greater sense of purpose.

Some of my happiest moments in the last few years have been with a guitar playing music with others.

# Stress reduction and emotional well-being

Creativity is a stress reliever and can improve overall mental and emotional well-being. When you are being successfully creative, whether playing music, painting a watercolor, or writing prose, you are in the moment. This is what sports psychologists call, "flow state". You may find yourself "in the zone" of this flow state at any time, while enjoying a pleasant stroll through the countryside, while being involved in a game of football, or even while knitting.

Creative endeavors frequently absorb you to the point that the outside world and time falls away. This is similar to the "mindfulness" of traditional meditation. There are a host of physical and mental benefits to being mindful, for example, your blood pressure comes down. Being in the flow state promotes greater well-being. Through creative pursuits, we can find outlets for expression, channel energy in a positive way, and experience this same sense of calm and relaxation. People will see you as charismatic. You'll be healthier, happier, and your relationships will improve.

## Enhanced life skills

Some of us thought our education stopped the moment we left school, university, or training. This isn't true. Education should happen throughout life.

Creativity nurtures critical thinking and problem-solving abilities. By engaging in creative endeavors, we can develop innovative approaches to challenges in our personal and professional lives. The process of creating something from idea to finished product requires a lot of steps. Whether you are composing music, writing text, or creating art, there are a million and one things to bear in mind to make your creation the best it can be. This is where the problem-solving and critical thinking brain muscles are exercised.

The ability to think outside the box and find unique solutions becomes an asset not only in creative pursuits but in other areas of life as well.

## Improved cognitive function and brain health

Numerous studies have shown a link between mental activities and improved cognitive function. Critical thinking and problem-solving are mental activities. This is why any sort of creative activity stimulates the brain, promoting neural plasticity. It can improve memory, concentration, and overall mental agility, reducing the risk of cognitive decline as we age. This is especially important for those of us who know they are genetically predisposed to Alzheimer's or other cognitive diseases linked to age.

## Boosted confidence and self-esteem

We have discussed how some people don't feel as though anyone is listening to them and are lacking self-esteem as a result.

Discovering or rediscovering your creative potential helps with confidence and self-esteem. There's no better feeling when someone congratulates you on your artistic skills or, even better, tells you how they've connected emotionally with your work. The sense of accomplishment is immense and inspires you to continue and make even better work.

## Increased resilience

Whilst being creative, you have to learn how to fail. And sometimes you'll fail epically, embarrassingly, and in public. This helps you cultivate resilience and adaptability. Creativity helps us embrace experimentation, learn from failures, and adapt to new situations.

## Increased socializing and connecting with people

The increased use of social media through a handheld device as well as increased individualism, has meant that we spend less time in the company of others than we used to.

Loneliness among young adults has been increasing since 1976. This is according to *Our Epidemic of Loneliness and Isolation*, the US Surgeon General's Advisory on the Healing Effects of Social Connection and Community. Adults in the US report having fewer close friends than they did in previous years, and the number of people living alone is also increasing.

And, then along came COVID-19. I was quite happy before the pandemic, playing guitar in bars and restaurants around town a few times a week. And, then, not only did all the bars and restaurants close, I also wouldn't have been allowed to play and sing even if the places were open. There were government directives that musicians and singers had to perform behind perspex screens (fortunately, that directive was short-lived). The pandemic really tested my resilience. I'm sure it tested yours. I'm thankfully back playing music with friends several nights a week now. And how I missed it!

But, for me, one of the worst results of the pandemic wasn't the isolation we felt during those maddening couple of years. But, sadly, some of the isolation has carried on as people developed new habits as a result. For example, I order and eat food at home more often now, whereas before the pandemic, I never did. So, these days I'm less likely to go to a local takeaway or shop to grab something to eat. A trip to the local restaurant would often result in a chat with the staff there or maybe I'd see someone I know and eat with them. It's one less chance to meet new friends.

There is no better way to connect with others than through creative pursuits. Through creativity, we can join artistic communities, collaborate on projects, or attend workshops or classes. This builds meaningful relationships that transcend age, background, or profession.

## Personal growth

In this book, I will not only encourage you to take up one creative hobby but a multitude of them. I will encourage you to blur the distinctions between creative disciplines. Musicians can incorporate elements of performance art into their shows; artists can incorporate elements of dramatic art into their exhibitions. This comes from the increased neural plasticity that creativity inspires. Creativity fosters a spirit of adaptability and promotes experimentation. At any stage in life, you can train your mind to be more creative.

So, for me, unleashing a spirit of creativity is as much about personal development as it is about the pure pleasure of creating. The exploration of new interests and hobbies will expand your skills, knowledge, and artistic capabilities, challenging you to constantly evolve and develop as an individual.

## Emotional intelligence and empathy

Unfortunately, the stresses and strains of many of our lives has caused a lot of negativity. Many people have embraced hate in order to come to terms with difficult situations. However, engaging in creative activities cultivates emotional intelligence and empathy. Often through creativity, you are putting yourself in someone else's shoes. A man singing Toni Braxton's *Un-break My Heart* would have to emote some female sensitivities in his performance.

By exploring different perspectives, characters, and emotions through creative expression, we delve deeper into our own emotions and those of others. This can enhance our ability to connect with and relate to all sorts of people on a deeper level. Emotional intelligence is a life skill which is important in all areas of life, not only in the creative sphere.

## Cathartic release and emotional healing

Many of us have been through hard times. Some people, because of past trauma, are suffering from PTSD. Sometimes our response is often to bottle up these harmful experiences and suppress the memories.

Creativity can serve as a cathartic outlet. People who channel their emotions into creative endeavors find solace and healing. I have always found playing my guitar and singing to be a healing activity. I have always sought comfort in music.

## Human-centric skills

There's no doubt that technological improvements in areas such as Artificial Intelligence and automation will take over certain jobs. And, for this reason, there is a growing need for human-centric skills, such as creativity, critical thinking, and problem-solving. Machines will ultimately paint "better" pictures than us, tell "better" stories than us, or make "better" music than us. But, machines will never be the quirky, creative, error-prone individuals than we are.

Creativity is the crucial distinguishing factor that sets individuals apart from machines. So, as jobs disappear because of new technology, we need creativity to add meaning to our lives. As new technology performs tasks better than we can, we need creativity for relevance.

## Unleashing the power of creativity: A journey of self-discovery

Creativity is not just for the talented, the lucky, and the rich. It's for everyone. It's a journey of self-discovery, a path to finding your voice in a society where some feel they don't have one. It's about expressing yourself, finding joy, and being in the moment. It's about being in the flow state, where the outside world and time fall away, and you are completely absorbed in your creative bliss.

Creativity is also about resilience. It's about learning how to fail, sometimes epically, embarrassingly, and in public. It's about embracing experimentation, learning from failures, and adapting to new situations. It's about developing innovative approaches to challenges in both personal and professional lives.

Creativity is about connection. It's about joining artistic communities, collaborating on projects, attending workshops or classes, and building meaningful relationships that transcend age, background, or profession. It's about exploring different perspectives, characters, and emotions, enhancing our ability to connect with and relate to all sorts of people on a deeper level.

Creativity is about healing. It's about channeling

emotions into creative endeavors and finding solace. It's about using creativity as a cathartic outlet, a way to release harmful experiences and suppressed memories.

Finally, creativity is about personal growth. It's about expanding skills, knowledge, and artistic capabilities, challenging you to constantly evolve and develop as an individual. It's about nurturing critical thinking and problem-solving abilities, improving memory, concentration, and overall mental agility.

So, let's embark on this journey together. Let's unleash the spirit of creativity and see where it takes us because creativity is not just about creating something beautiful. It's also about creating a beautiful life.

# Isaac Newton

Isaac Newton was born in Woolsthorpe, Lincolnshire, England, in 1643. He showed exceptional intelligence and curiosity from a young age. As a student at the University of Cambridge, his brilliance was obvious, particularly in mathematics and physics.

During 1665 and 1666, England was struck by a deadly, unknown illness, known as The Great Plague, and Newton's university closed its doors. He was therefore isolated in his family estate where, with nothing much else to do, he immersed himself in his studies. It was during this time that the apple incident, often associated with his discovery, is said to have taken place.

Sitting in the garden one day, Newton noticed an apple fall from a tree. This mundane event sparked thoughts in his creative mind. He thought, "why did that apple fall straight down and not sideways or upwards?" This simple observation ignited his curiosity about the force behind the apple's motion.

Drawing on his previous studies of mathematics and physics, Newton started to explore the possibility of a universal force that governed the motion of celestial bodies and everyday objects on Earth. He envisioned a force that extended throughout space and influenced the behavior of all objects, regardless of their size.

Newton's creative insight led him to develop the

theory of gravity. He postulated that every particle of matter in the universe exerted an attractive force on every other particle, and this force decreased with distance. Moreover, he proposed that the strength of the gravitational force was directly proportional to the mass of the objects involved.

Over the following years, Newton worked tirelessly to refine his theory. His groundbreaking publication, "Philosophiæ Naturalis Principia Mathematica" (Mathematical Principles of Natural Philosophy), released in 1687, presented his theory of gravity along with his laws of motion. This monumental work laid the foundation for classical mechanics and revolutionized the field of physics.

Newton's creative insight into the theory of gravity not only explains why objects fall to the ground but also explains the motion of celestial bodies, such as the moon and planets. His theory became a cornerstone of scientific understanding.

Isaac Newton's revolutionary insight not only changed our perception of the physical world but also inspired countless scientists and thinkers to explore the depths of the universe and uncover its mysteries.

# Step one: Unblock the blocks, rekindle the creative flame, and ignite inspiration

Our lives in this early part of the twentieth century are dominated by routine. We may be expected to provide income for ourselves and our families, look after and transport children, and provide support and care for elderly parents or relatives.

Regardless of our routine, when we do have any spare time on our hands, we will be expected by society to engage in more practical or relaxing hobbies. After a hard week working whilst caring for a sick mother in the evenings, you'd expect someone to spend their weekend relaxing with the television, not producing watercolor paintings of lilies.

If someone had never painted watercolors before, they will naturally compare themselves to a great watercolor artist who has a helpful channel on YouTube. Inevitably, they will presume the gulf between their current artistic ability and the artistic ability that is anywhere good enough is just too vast.

Furthermore, we are increasingly isolated these days. As we enter adulthood, we may find that old friends have left town. Maybe we were forced to leave our hometown for work. So, we are left on our own. We don't have that support circle. A strong supportive social network can be essential for encouragement and collaboration.

We have been disconnected not only from a support network but also from a creative outlet. Maybe we played the drums when in high school, maybe we wrote short stories while young, but we haven't done anything remotely creative for decades as life's demands took over. Now, we must find the energy and time for creativity with a self-perceived "skill gap" as it's been ages since we followed our passions.

"I would love to be drumming in a band again but I haven't done it for years! I'll be rusty and out of practice. What's the point?" We've heard these self-defeating statements before. It's natural for us to compare ourselves to others or even to ourselves in the past and feel that we would come up short.

In reality, past experience is "money in the bank that's gaining interest". Sure, you may be a bit rusty if you haven't played the drums for a few years. But your sense of rhythm will still be there. And the muscle memory and coordination has also remained. It just needs to be brought back to life.

It's also natural that adults will have quite settled habits. Maybe they will go to the same restaurant every weekend. They'll always watch the same shows on TV. They'll listen to the same music they listened to in their earlier years. "Music was better in those days." (Disclaimer: I'm Gen X myself and I totally agree with that last statement.) "I know what music I like, so what's the point of discovering other types of music? Anyway, I hate the music I hear other people listening to half the time!"

This is understandable to me. Because I have said the above statements many times in the last few years. But the truth is that there is a lot of good music out there. You just have to search for it. It's not surprising that there's a lot of bad music around—there always was. We just can't hear it with the rose tinted earplugs we've placed in our ears.

Regardless, in our busy lives, we have limited exposure to inspiration. When was the last time you went to an art gallery and gasped at the beauty of a painting from nineteenth century Europe? In my case, it was 40 years ago.

The free time that we have to experience "culture" is spent scrolling Facebook or YouTube timelines, which presents us with content that will either make us angry or frightened, or both. That's hardly inspirational. When did you last see something truly beautiful on social media?

So, we've got people with little time on their hands, a limited support network, societal pressures, self-doubt, a self-perceived skill gap, and are lacking inspiration.

Well, I guess we better give up then. What's the point of me writing this book? All that harking back to the past, where you were truly happy and in the zone indulging in a creative activity you absolutely loved, is just a waste of time. A happy memory. But just that. Stop dreaming and get back to the practical grind! We are all doomed and will never experience the joys of creativity ever again.

Forgive me, I'm joking.

All the above challenges are just that, challenges. All these challenges can be overcome. We'll just have to … get creative!

The reasons you believe you've lost the creative spark or the reasons you think you'll never enjoy a creative passion are … all in your head.

I can unblock these obstacles one by one.

## Finding time

We all have our obligations. But there are many ways you can find time to be creative and still have as much time for work and relaxation.

You need to prioritize creativity. This will include being self-disciplined in what you allow yourself to do and not to do. It's quite possible you don't realize how much time you spend on unproductive and uncreative activities.

These unproductive and uncreative activities may include watching TV or aimless internet browsing, etc. So, you could practice "mindful technology use". The algorithms behind the timelines we engage with can give us addictive dopamine fixes throughout the day. These dopamine fixes will stop us from requiring the dopamine fixes from creativity. Be mindful of how you engage with technology. Consider implementing guidelines for its usage or set aside "tech-free" periods during your day to create space. Creatives need space.

We all need time to unwind. Watching a half-decent Netflix series before bedtime is a near perfect way to end the day. And, to be creative, you need time to rest and recuperate. You can do this by eliminating some activities that are taking up too much of your time and, potentially, harming you.

Is it possible to "delegate" some of your obligations? Can another relative help you with your care duties? Can you pretend you're sick so you can't meet your friends for dinner this weekend?

Kaizen is a Japanese word which means "good change". Kaizen is a practice of enacting small incremental changes regularly. After a while, these tiny incremental changes can yield big results. Maybe just practicing your chosen creative pursuit for just ten minutes a day at first. You could implement the Japanese practice of Kaizen into your creative goals.

There are lots you can do to manage your time more effectively. Another example is to create a time log and keep a record of how you spend your free time. It may be surprising to see how many hours a week you spend flicking through a timeline, for example.

However, I would urge caution here. Different

character types respond differently to the same stimuli. Some people (especially "creative types") don't respond too well to discipline and routine. I know I don't. So, don't be too hard on yourself, especially when you're just starting out. We need to preserve time for relaxation every day. We're not machines.

Journaling and goal setting are two pillars of time management. We will explore them later on in this book.

Don't allow time constraints to stand between you and your potential.

## Challenge what is expected of you

As adults, we are expected to be practical and effective, not creative and experimental. You need to challenge this societal expectation. Shift your mindset, and the mindset of those around you.

Embrace the idea that creativity is a valuable and fulfilling pursuit. More important than the ability to fix a bust water faucet.

Remind yourself and others that it's important to explore and express your passions, regardless of traditional expectations.

## Overcoming self-doubt and fear of judgment

Some of the most accomplished artists and successful people suffer from self-doubt so you must take your own fears with a pinch of salt.

You're not going to create the most beautiful pieces of art when you're starting out. It's essential that you realize that creativity is a personal journey and it's okay to make mistakes. Remember why you're doing this. It's the joy and fulfillment that comes from the creative process itself. Embrace your mistakes. They're how you learn.

Learn to love your mistakes and love the process. Creativity can be learned. It's not all about innate talent. Feel this in your bones. This growth mindset can also be learned.

Seek out all learning opportunities, not just in your creative discipline, but everywhere. Even if you want to reignite your passion for music, don't limit yourself to music. Try a little art every now and again. All creativity comes from the same place and creatives often appreciate and spend time outside their chosen discipline. The list of musicians and actors who are/were also artists is as long as it is diverse: David Bowie, John Lennon, Joni Mitchell, Anthony Hopkins, Jim Carrey, Jane Seymour, I could go on. Be the same as these people. This is not only how you nurture creativity. It's also how you seek out the growth mindset.

Again, self-doubt and negative self-judgment can be tempered by a community of like-minded individuals. We will talk more about this in other sections of the book. There is a huge benefit to seeking out fellow creatives who appreciate and encourage you.

## Finding a support network

If you believe you don't have a support network at the moment, you may think it's a daunting task to suddenly create one. It may be that you already know individuals that also would like to reignite a creative streak, you've just never asked them about it.

Share your creative interests with friends, family, and loved ones. You may be surprised at their reaction. Everyone enjoys creativity in some way so people will be genuinely interested. And maybe someone you know will pipe up and say, 'you know, I'd love to get into painting portraits.' You could then ask them to join an informal support group. You could offer them advice and feedback and, in return, take advice and feedback from them. It doesn't matter if their chosen creative path is different from yours.

You can also actively seek out individuals who share your creative interests online. Have a look for forums on the Internet generally as well as on various social media. Join art groups, attend workshops, or participate in online forums where you can share your work and receive constructive feedback in a supportive environment.

Whenever you meet creative individuals who you're impressed by, *tell them they're awesome.* Express sincere and honest praise to other creatives. Don't be embarrassed. You know how difficult it is to "put yourself out there" creatively. Everyone finds it difficult. So when someone has, not only, got past their blocks, but also has done it well, then they are worthy of praise. Always try to be positive. Even if it's someone you don't know well. Compliments start positive relationships. And you need as many positive relationships as you can get.

Always be positive; never be negative.

There is probably more of a creative support network around you than you actually realize, but it has to be nurtured.

## Seeking out like-minded individuals

It is most important not to travel on your creative journey alone. You may start off on your own but you should seek to collaborate with like-minded individuals as soon as you can.

If you are embarking on writing a classic in your attic now you may be wondering how on earth you can collaborate with other writers. But, I would still encourage those who are engaged in the most solitary creative pursuits to go out, meet and engage with other people who share your creative passions. In fact, I know of writers who meet weekly to write together for a few hours and then mix socially.

Meeting people who are feeling the same creative birthing pains as you can be therapeutic, if nothing less. But it can also be encouraging, stimulating, and inspiring.

All blues and jazz musicians, ultimately, have to seek out others to feed their creativity. They can't do certain things on their own. So some creatives are forced to go out there and collaborate. But all creatives should go out there and share their creativity.

During the course of writing this book, I have searched online for various groups for specific endeavors. They are out there. Whatever your creative endeavor, your first online port of call will be Google, Facebook, and Meetup.com. These may be fruitless. You may not find organizations but not in your hometown. But it's worth a try. And, if you can't find an online group, you can create one yourself.

If you're engaged in visual arts, then I would encourage you to post all your artworks online, however experimental. As I've said already, you should seek out others posting online and compliment those people who you truly admire. You may consider them to be unapproachable, but they probably don't see themselves that way. It's quite possible for you to strike up an enduring friendship online. Even online collaboration can spark new ideas, provide feedback, and enhance your creative process. Ask for feedback and give feedback, when it's constructive.

But there's a flip side to this. You may, sadly, be experiencing negativity from certain people. I'm afraid this is part of life. Some people who are going through a bad time will want to put you down for trying something new. They don't feel capable of trying something new at this present moment and they are touchy about their lack of achievement. This will unfortunately present itself as a tendency to put down anyone who tries a new pursuit or anything different from the failure that they've grown accustomed to. It is essential that you ignore these people and don't let them succeed in pulling you down to their level. They will heal in time. But, until then, give them a wide berth.

Forming deep relationships with a group of supportive people is one of the prerequisites to a happy, healthy, and productive life. One of the main reasons for the depression and isolation that individuals feel in these trying times is that they don't have a support network. Try to consistently nurture your support network.

## Finding inspiration

Another roadblock in the way of creativity is a lack of exposure to various forms of art. You may have forgotten the last time you visited an art gallery or a museum. Maybe you believe that you've already visited these places in your local area, so there's no point in going again. It's quite possible that they've changed since you went there. Unfortunately, COVID-19 and the digital revolution caused people to spend less time experiencing these places. Creatives should buck this trend. It may be that your local museum or art space has changed their expositions since you last visited them. While you're there, you may find some inspiration.

By the same token, you could deliberately expose yourself to different art forms. Go see bands playing styles of music you don't usually listen to. Read fiction books of the type you don't usually read. Watch movies from countries other than the United States. (And, yes, that means reading subtitles). There are lots of things offline you can do to broaden your artistic horizons and spark new ideas.

Sadly, many of us will look back on our lives and lament our lack of creativity. This will compare badly with how we were in our childhood, teens, and twenties. Why do we expect people to suddenly stop being creative as they advance toward their thirties and beyond?

You are entitled to claim or reclaim your creativity at any time in your life. However, there are many activities you can actively participate in to make sure your new creative urge is not short-lived.

## Rediscovering old hobbies

If you used to play the guitar or any other instrument, you're in luck. The instruments haven't changed in the last hundred years, but Google, YouTube, and online learning is now here to help you.

This is exactly the same whether you used to be a writer, a poet, a photographer or some sort of artist. The content available online to help you pick up or restart a hobby is immense.

When I was learning guitar in the late 70s and early 80s, I had to go to a music shop to buy sheet music for a particular song in order to discover how a song was played. Or I could spend hours with a guitar and a tape machine laboriously playing along with the track. Now, an aficionado will demonstrate exactly how to master the piece of music I'm interested in. The YouTuber might then suggest different ways to play the song, suggest other songs or techniques that would also be interesting to play, and encourage me to try more challenging tutorials.

And, of course, the same goes for any creative discipline. Whatever your interest, whether it be photography, writing, drawing, sculpting, dance, pottery, woodwork, calligraphy, graphic design, collage art, puppetry, or journalling, there'll be an enthusiast creating free content to help you connect with it. This might not sound earth-shattering as we've all become accustomed to the convenience and ubiquity of the Internet over the last few years. But it is, I think, game changing.

## Creating a home studio

If you can, set up a small area of your home dedicated to your chosen creative pursuit or pursuits. If you are a musician, you could invest in basic recording equipment and software that allows you to produce your own music.

Or, if you intend to engage with art, pick an area of your home with good natural light where you can create or experiment with your creative visions.

This will not be possible for people like me who live in small apartments. But I also have access to practice studios in my local area where I can indulge in my favored creative pursuit for a small cost.

Whatever way you decide on, realize that creativity can come from anywhere. Whether you are alone or collaborating, whether you are in your special creative space or out and about, you are entitled to explore your creative urges wherever you are.

## Self-reflection and self-evaluation

Take time to reflect on your creative journey. Look how far you've come.

Evaluate your strengths as well as areas for improvement. Self-reflection helps you better understand your creative process and identify areas where you can evolve.

Continually push yourself to be better at your craft. A creative journal will help you here.

## Playfulness and experimentation

Playfulness and experimentation are not characteristics that society would associate with adults. But they should be. Playfulness and experimentation are second nature to children and no one questions why children enjoy themselves playing.

But, look at the artists, musicians, and writers who enjoyed success in their twenties but never managed to recreate the spark of their peak performance.

However, as I've seen in my mid-50s, I'm a better guitarist, bassist, singer, harmoniser, artist, and writer than I was at any other time in my life. I would never have realized this unless I experimented by picking up the guitar again to tediously relearn skills I'd mastered thirty years previously, and then subsequently, to exceed them.

I only started creating YouTube videos and writing books after my 40th birthday. What the hell was I doing in my thirties? Working and commuting in London was enough to annihilate my playfulness and experimentation.

Try to cultivate a sense of playfulness and curiosity in your life in general. Allow yourself to think stupid things. Allow yourself to fail playfully. Experiment with new endeavors without fear of judgment. Embrace playfulness and exploration and doors to new worlds will open.

## Nurture a non-judgmental life

It follows that you should be in an environment where creativity, playfulness, and experimentation are possible. You may not feel like playing when you're tired, stressed, and suffering from a hangover. Maybe you live in close proximity to people who are putting you down and don't understand your creative urges.

Block off the negative areas of your life. Sure, we all need to work or do things we don't love doing. But, it is possible to keep these negative areas of your life to a minimum. Get them over and done with as soon as possible and don't judge. And then go to your creative place and close the door behind you.

With creativity, everything is on the table. The only way you can experiment, play, create, make mistakes, learn, and grow as a human being is without judgment. So, ignore the judgments that come your way, and be at peace in your bliss.

## Draw from personal experiences

What do you create your art about? This is the easiest question to answer. If you are an author, you write about your life. If you are an artist, you draw inspiration from yourself. If you are a musician, you sing about your own pain. You create your art about yourself.

No matter what your creative discipline, the challenges and triumphs of your own personal experience is the primary source of creative fuel.

We've all had traumas, trials, and tribulations. And rather than stewing in bitterness about the bad periods, creating art about them and challenging your emotions through your work is a cathartic and healing process.

This is the human condition. Life is bound to throw you a curveball, especially when you least expect it. We've all felt blighted by extra bad luck as well as enjoying extreme pleasures in our lives. And, those that tell life stories that resonate with others have been some of the world's most successful artists.

## Actionable takeaways

- **Challenge Societal Expectations**: Embrace the idea that creativity is a valuable and fulfilling pursuit. Remind yourself and others that it's important to explore and express your passions, regardless of traditional expectations.
- **Manage Your Time Effectively**: Implement practices like journaling and goal setting to manage your time more effectively. I'll help you with this later in the book. Create a time log and keep a record of how you spend your free time.
- **Find Your Creative Space**: Whether you are alone or collaborating, whether you are in your special creative space or out and about, you are entitled to

explore your creative urges wherever you are.
- **Self-Reflection and Self-Evaluation**: Take time to reflect on your creative journey. Look how far you've come. Evaluate your strengths as well as areas for improvement. Self-reflection helps you better understand your creative process and identify areas where you can evolve.
- **Playfulness and Experimentation**: Embrace playfulness and experimentation. These are not characteristics that society would associate with adults. But they should be. Playfulness and experimentation are second nature to children and no one questions why children enjoy themselves so much.
- **Finding Inspiration**: Deliberately expose yourself to different art forms. Go see bands playing styles of music you don't usually listen to. Read fiction books of the type you don't usually read. Watch movies from countries other than the United States. There are lots of things offline you can do to broaden your artistic horizons and spark new ideas.

Remember, you are entitled to claim or reclaim your creativity at any time in your life. However, there are many activities you can actively do to manage your time more effectively.

# Richard Adams

Richard Adams was born on May 9, 1920, in Newbury, Berkshire, England. He worked in the British Civil Service for most of his adult life.

After his graduation in 1948, which was delayed by the Second World War, Adams joined the British Civil Service, rising to the rank of Assistant Secretary to the Ministry of Housing and Local Government.

He used to tell stories to his young daughters during long car journeys to keep them amused. He started with a story about rabbits, one of them with extra-sensory perception. He later reported that the stories came "from the top of his head". But his children insisted he write them down. Later, he began to write in his spare time, reading them to his children and later on, to his grandchildren.

Initially, Adams struggled to find a publisher for his manuscript. Finally, in 1972, when he was 52, and after countless rejections, Adams secured a publishing deal for *Watership Down* with Rex Collings Ltd.

*Watership Down* resonated with readers of all ages. Adams' remarkable storytelling prowess, combined with his deep understanding of the natural world, transported readers into a vividly imagined rabbit society.

The success of *Watership Down* catapulted Adams into literary stardom. The novel received critical acclaim, won numerous awards and has sold over 50 million copies. Adams went on to write several more novels, including "Shardik" and "The Plague Dogs".

Richard Adams' story shows that creativity knows no age limits. His journey from the world of civil service to becoming a celebrated author in his fifties reminds us that it is never too late to pursue our passions and share our uniqueness with the world.

# Step two: Pleasure and business

You could say that there are two sides to creativity. Business and pleasure. Sometimes, we indulge in creative pastimes for pure pleasure. And, sometimes, our creativity makes us a living.

But it's not black and white. Business and pleasure merge into one another.

Some of us may invest significant time into a creative pastime with only a little financial return, which may be viewed as unproductive from a strictly business perspective. Whereas others, like Richard Adams, the author of *Watership Down*, sold millions of copies of a story he told his daughters to keep them amused during a long car journey.

We'll never know where our creativity will take us.

In this chapter, I want to address the age old conundrum of how to balance business and pleasure. How much importance do we give to our creative pastimes versus using creativity for business and making a living?

## Prioritize passion

If you want to improve your muscles, you train with weights. If you want to improve your fitness, you do cardiovascular exercise. If you want to improve your cognition, you exercise your brain as often and as vigorously as you can.

Creativity is the same. You have to practice it. And keep at it. Luckily, our creativity and neural pathways, in most cases, remain responsive to training into advanced old age, unlike our bodies.

You have to dedicate time to your creative passions and your creative endeavors for business. You also have your other daily obligations and tasks. Sounds too difficult? It isn't. Not if you can creatively adapt.

Goal setting is incredibly important in business. Show me a business without goals and it'll be a failing business. The same is true for your creative passions.

If you are hoping your creativity will one day earn you a living or become a productive side hustle, goals are even more important. You may love, as I do, creating designs for T-shirts. Or maybe, like me, you love writing. But if you want these passions to make you money, you need goals. Set yourself the goal of creating 50 T-shirt designs and uploading them to an online platform by a certain time. Or set yourself the goal of writing a blog post or a social media update every week.

One of the goals I've set myself recently is to be able to improvise a decent solo on guitar over a moderate tempo 12 bar blues backing track. Should these goals be time sensitive? Yes.

The difference between the business and pleasure goals is that in business you have an "audience" whose reaction can be measured and incorporated into the goal. With pleasure, the goal is really up to you to define. But, if you want to make money, you need feedback to see if you're on the right track. If I'm goal setting for my 12 bars blues solo, I have to be happy with it and that's enough. However if I'm setting goals for creative business, it's not just about me. I have to make other people happy as well, not just myself.

So, of those 50 T-shirt designs, how many sold? What engagement are you getting on your blog posts or social media updates? If these measurable audience reactions are moving in the right direction, then you can create more goals. Upload more T-shirts, write more social media posts, etc. But, if your creative business endeavors aren't being met with audience approval, you need to re-evaluate.

There are different timeframes of goals you can set yourself as well. There are tasks you need to do by the end of the week. There are monthly, quarterly, annual goals. And big fat hairy goals that you could aim for in a number of years.

This is where the creative journal that is discussed elsewhere in this book comes to the fore. A goal is not a goal if it's not written down. You should have multiple goals of differing timescales and they should be tailored to the business or pleasure nature of the activity.

# Financial considerations

Evaluate the financial aspects of your creative pursuits. Consider whether you want to prioritize making a living solely from your creative endeavors or if you prefer to maintain a day job. Finding a balance that suits your financial needs and creative fulfillment is key.

# Flexibility

You've got to get creative with your creativity! Don't worry too much about the time constraints on the goals or even the goals themselves. They are there for focus and prioritization. If you fail at your goals, it doesn't mean that they aren't any less important than the goals you succeeded in.

And don't be too strict with yourself with the dedicated time you've set for each of your creative passions. If you've blocked off a couple of hours for writing but you've sat in front of a blank screen for a few minutes and it's just not happening, get up and do something else.

Creativity is all about flexibility. Creative thinking is being able to see something that has never been seen before. Indulge in "idea sex". Put two ideas together and see what comes up. Jumping quickly between different creative tasks builds new neural pathways in the brain and makes you more adaptable.

I would encourage you to pick several, not one,

## Enjoy yourself

Ultimately, this book is about making you happy. Creativity is to be enjoyed. Allow yourself the freedom to explore new creative avenues both for pleasure and business. This can help prevent burnout and keep your creativity fresh and exciting. Experimentation can lead to unexpected discoveries and opportunities for growth in both realms.

## Actionable takeaways

- **Balance Business and Pleasure**: Creativity has two sides, business and pleasure. Sometimes, we indulge in creative pastimes for pure pleasure, and sometimes, our creativity makes us a living. It's important to find a balance between these two aspects.
- **Prioritize Passion**: Dedicate time to your creative passions and your creative endeavors for business. Creativity, like any other skill, needs to be practiced and nurtured.
- **Set Goals**: Goal setting is incredibly important in business and for your creative passions. Write down your goals and have multiple goals of differing timescales.
- **Evaluate Financial Aspects**: Consider whether you want to prioritize making a living solely from your creative endeavors or if you prefer to maintain a day

creative tasks to complete each day and jump, quickly and thoughtlessly, from one task to the next as the fancy takes you. This is a great way to enhance your creative thinking while being creative at the same time.

## Reflection

Nothing is set in stone. These are suggestions for you to adopt if you think they fit for you. And sometimes, attitudes and regimens will work, and other times, they won't.

This is why creatives will regularly reflect on the balance between business and pleasure in their lives. We need to assess whether we feel fulfilled in both areas and make adjustments as needed.

Everything is change. Be open to re-evaluating your priorities and making changes that align with your evolving self.

Two essential tools in the creative toolbox will help with this: meditation and journaling. I will write about these two disciplines in the next chapter. I don't mean that meditation should be about self-reflection. You shouldn't be actively self-reflecting while meditating. While meditating, your mind will ideally be clear of all thoughts as you non-judgmentally concentrate on the present moment. But after extensive meditation, self-reflection will come to you more naturally. Ideas will pop into your head more readily because you've created space for them.

job to support your creative passions for pleasure.
- **Be Flexible**: Creativity is all about flexibility. Don't be too strict with yourself with the dedicated time you've set for each of your creative passions. If you're not feeling creative, do something else.
- **Experiment**: Jump quickly between different creative tasks. This builds new neural pathways in the brain and makes you more adaptable.
- **Reflect Regularly**: Reflect on the balance between business and pleasure in your life. Be open to re-evaluating your priorities and making changes that align with your evolving self.
- **Enjoy Yourself**: Allow yourself the freedom to explore new creative avenues both for pleasure and business. This can help prevent burnout and keep your creativity fresh and exciting.

Remember, these are suggestions for you to adopt if you think they fit for you. The balance between business and pleasure in creativity will vary from person to person, and so it's important to find what works best for you.

# Taikichiro Mori

Taikichiro Mori was born in 1904, in Tokyo. Mori built a successful career in the world of real estate. However, it wasn't until his 60s that he discovered a new passion that would bring him immense joy and artistic expression: photography.

Throughout his life, Mori had always possessed a deep appreciation for the visual arts. He admired the beauty and intricacies of the world around him, and it was this fascination that eventually led him to pick up a camera and capture his vision.

In his 60s, Mori embarked on a new chapter of his life by dedicating himself to the practice of photography. With his keen eye for composition and an innate ability to capture fleeting moments, he quickly realized that this medium allowed him to convey emotions, stories, and perspectives in a way that resonated with him.

Mori's photographs began to garner attention and acclaim within artistic circles. His work showcased a remarkable blend of creativity, sensitivity, and a profound connection with the world around him. Through his lens, he captured the beauty of nature, the energy of urban landscapes, and the essence of the human experience.

As his photographic portfolio expanded, Mori's reputation as a talented artist grew. His images were exhibited in renowned galleries and museums.

Mori's late-in-life pursuit of photography brought him immeasurable fulfillment and personal satisfaction. Through this creative medium, he found an avenue for self-expression, a way to connect with others, and a source of continuous learning and growth.

# Step three: Groundwork

The following are some suggestions of things you can do right now to exercise your creative muscles.

## Meditation

Meditation is non-judgmental awareness of the present moment. You may not think meditation can be described as a creative act. But I wanted to start this chapter off with meditation because it is central to what I'm trying to achieve with this book—greater creativity, awareness, and happiness.

Meditation will clear your mind, which will leave space for creativity. And, furthermore, when one is absorbed in creativity, whether one is writing prose, singing, painting, etc., one is also engaged in non-judgmental present moment concentration—i.e., meditation.

Here's a closer look at the benefits.

By concentrating on the present moment, instead of stressing about the past and future and calming the mind, your heart rate decreases, your breathing slows down, your blood pressure drops. Mindfulness and meditation can help reduce stress and anxiety.

Mindfulness and meditation practices train the mind to stay present and focused. This improved concentration can help artists and creators immerse themselves fully in the creative process, leading to greater clarity of thought and attention to detail.

Individuals who practice meditation and mindfulness cultivate an open and non-judgmental attitude. This allows for different perspectives, the ability to see things from different angles, and the potential for creative breakthroughs.

Focussing on the present moment rather than worrying about future outcomes or past experiences frees you from self-judgment and perfectionism. This will therefore allow you to fully engage in the creative process and enjoy the journey itself.

So, how does one meditate?

- **Find a quiet and comfortable space**: Choose a quiet place where you can sit comfortably without distractions. It could be a designated meditation area or any peaceful spot in your home.
- **Assume a comfortable posture**: Sit in a posture that is both relaxed and alert. Sit upright on a chair with your feet flat on the ground. Keep your spine upright but not rigid. Do not pick a chair with a support for your head. Instead, make sure your head is resting comfortably and centrally on your shoulders.
- **Set a time limit**: If you are new to the practice, I would start with a 3 to 5 minute meditation. You'll want to increase the time limit after 5 minutes becomes easy. Try to meditate at the same time of the day every day. First thing in the morning is best.
- **Focus on your breathing**: Close your eyes or softly

gaze towards where the horizon would be. Allow your breath to flow naturally. Direct your attention to the sensation of your breath. Be aware of the physical sensations in your body, the inhalation and exhalation, the rise and fall of your abdomen, or the feeling of air on the insides of your nostrils. If you are a beginner, concentrate on the nostrils first.

- **No one is a perfect meditator**. You will be amazed by how difficult it is to concentrate on the present moment for even a few seconds at first! Thoughts and distractions will arise. Acknowledge them without judgment and gently let them go, returning your attention to the breath. It's normal for the mind to wander, and each time it does, simply bring it back to the present moment.
- **Slowly open your eyes**: When you're finished, allow yourself a moment to "transition" before getting up and carrying on with your day.

Meditation is a personal practice. Over time, you will hopefully notice the benefits of increased calmness in your daily life. I did at first. I've also had periods when it hasn't been working for me as I wanted it to. Take it easy and don't judge yourself if it's not working out for you at first.

There are other types of meditation you can try as well but I would recommend silent sitting meditation for newcomers. Here are a few suggestions for different meditations you can do. Go through them and see which one resonates with you. Any of these will clear your head and minimize distractions, preparing you for the creative act.

**Gratitude meditation**: Take a few moments to reflect on the positive people, experiences, and resources that contribute to your day. Feel gratitude for all that is good in your life. You could do this after you have finished your silent/sitting meditation or at any moment in the day. For example, whilst enjoying a nice hot drink. Wake up in the morning and ruminate on how much you will enjoy breakfast.

**Loving-kindness meditation**: Extend loving-kindness towards yourself and others. Think of yourself first. Wish yourself good physical, mental, and spiritual health. Then think of those close to you. Wish them good physical, mental, and spiritual health. Then think of the people in your apartment block, next door, on your street, or in your neighborhood. Wish them good physical, mental, and spiritual health. Broaden out the group of people to include the area you live in, then the country you live in, then the continent, then the whole world. Send positive thoughts and well-wishes to all sentient beings on Earth. Acknowledge the interconnectedness of humanity. Again, you could do this after you have finished your silent/sitting meditation or at any moment in the day. Ideally, try to practice loving-kindness meditation when you are relaxed and in a quiet place.

**Mindful observation**: This is an advanced form of meditation that I've never tried. But if you are a painter or a visual artist, this may be useful for you. Sit in a quiet place and choose an object, such as a flower or a piece of artwork. Practice deep observation by noticing every detail, color, texture, and shape. Let your mind fully engage with the object and observe any creative thoughts or associations that arise.

Basic sitting meditation is enough. And increased calmness and clarity will help you in your creative endeavors, and in your life in general. If you take one thing from this book, make it this section about meditation.

# Mind Mapping

Mind mapping is a visual technique that helps organize and connect ideas, concepts, and information. It involves creating a diagram or map that starts with a central idea or topic and branches out into related subtopics and associations. The central idea is placed in the center of the map, and subsequent ideas are added as branches radiating out from it. Each branch represents a different aspect or subtopic, which can further branch out into more specific details or related ideas.

The alternative to mind mapping is to create boring linear lists. Mind mapping encourages three dimensional thinking where different concepts can be more easily connected. It's easier to see connections between different areas of a large visual diagram than it is in a linear list.

Using mind maps or brainstorming techniques can help stimulate creative thinking and generate new ideas. Mind mapping encourages free-flowing thinking, association of ideas, and the discovery of unexpected connections. This will enhance your creativity and enable you to come up with new ideas.

**Topic exploration**: This is basic mind mapping to get you started. Choose a broad topic that interests you and create a mind map to explore all the subtopics and ideas associated with it. Use branches to expand on each subtopic and capture related thoughts and connections. An example of this would be the mind map I created to write this book. I put "Enhance Your Creativity" in the center and drew a circle around it. I then drew lines off the center circle to other main concepts in the book (chapters). Other lines are drawn off from the concepts, creating secondary concepts (the subheadings within the chapters). The mind map changed while writing as I could connect chapters to ensure a logical narrative and cut down repetition. I regularly referred back to it while writing this book.

**Problem-solving challenge**: Identify a specific problem you're facing and use mind mapping to generate as many potential solutions or ideas as possible. Let your mind flow freely without judgment and explore unconventional or unexpected solutions.

**Goal setting**: Use mind mapping to define and visualize your goals. Start with a central goal or aspiration, and branch out to identify specific actions, resources, or steps needed to achieve it. Use colors, symbols, and images to make the mind map more visually motivating.

**Creative writing spark**: For whatever type of prose you are writing, start with a mind map as a tool in order to plan your project. Start with the central theme, plot, or character and branch out to explore various other characters, sub-themes, plotlines, or story ideas related to that.

**Decision-making exercise**: If you find decision-making difficult, you can use mind mapping to visually map out the pros, cons, and potential outcomes of each option. Put the difficult question in the middle of the mind map and branch off with all the potential options. This will help you clarify your thoughts and make a more informed decision.

**Mind maps for personal development**: You can use mind maps to explore different areas of personal development, such as health, relationships, career, or hobbies. Create branches for specific goals, habits, resources, or actions you can take to grow and improve in each area. This will give you new avenues for self improvement.

**Brainstorming for a project**: When starting a new creative project, create a mind map to generate ideas, potential strategies, and creative approaches. Use branches to explore different aspects of the project, such as target audience, timelines, research, or marketing tactics.

- How to Brainstorm with Mind Maps - Mindmaps.com https://www.mindmaps.com/how-to-brainstorm-with-mind-maps/

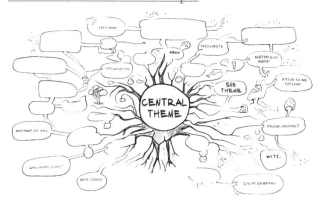

## Journaling

If you're not currently journaling, I would advise you to start today. The benefits are numerous. Journaling can crystallize your creative ideas and provide focus for your creativity as well as being a great way to get your thoughts in order.

I restarted journaling a couple of years ago and I have definitely experienced mental health benefits as a result of the practice.

Journaling is proven to reduce stress. When you journal, you write about what was good about your day.

This encourages gratitude. It's better to concentrate on what you have than what you don't have and that's why grateful people are happy. Think of what you ate this morning. It was tasty. It made you happier. That's just one example. When you journal, you write about the things you really love all the time, making you aware of what you have as opposed to what you don't have.

But, there's a flipside to that. You also tend to write about what you don't like. If there was a situation with a person that made you uncomfortable, you'll likely write about that in your journal. This helps you to process difficult emotions. It puts space around your negative thoughts because you get them out of your head and onto the page of your journal, freeing up valuable headspace. I often find meditation very difficult after a few days without journaling. That's because I haven't processed the negative situations of the past few days and they are still roaming around my consciousness making it hard for me to concentrate. Journaling closes your mental browser tabs. You can also journal about your creative endeavors.

**Gratitude journaling**: Write down three things you are grateful for each day. This could be anything: the cup of coffee you had in the morning; the pleasantries you exchanged with someone at a shop; a beautiful flower you saw on your walk home. Record the things that bring you joy and appreciation. This will soothe your soul, readying yourself for creativity.

**Stream of consciousness**: I remember reading Virginia Wolff's *To The Lighthouse* and being exasperated by the writing style but don't let that put you off. Virginia Wolff's highly original and influential writing inspired a generation of modernist authors. What is a stream of consciousness? It's where you write continuously without censoring or judging your thoughts. You just write. Allow your mind to wander freely on the page, expressing whatever comes to mind without limitations.

It's a bit like sitting down to play guitar and just riffing, noodling or strumming around without any particular song or direction in mind. You may go somewhere interesting, you may not. That's not the point. The point is to put whatever is inside you to the outside. That is, essentially, what creativity is all about.

**Vision journaling**: Engage in vision journaling by writing about your aspirations, dreams, and goals. I have already spoken of the need to set creative goals as a way to prioritize your passions. You can journal about the goals you have set for yourself in your chosen creative disciplines. Set goal completion dates and write about how these goals will come to fruition. You could also use visualization techniques to imagine and describe your ideal future.

## Actionable takeaways

Overall, these strategies provide a groundwork for

enhancing creativity. By implementing these strategies, you will see an improvement in your creative thinking and output.

I'd like to emphasize the importance of meditation as a tool to clear the mind and create space for creativity. I would also urge you to practice mindfulness, focusing on the present moment whenever you can.

Meditation is best practiced at the same time of the day, everyday. Ideally, I like to do it after waking up and showering before I've looked at my phone. You only need to sit down in a darkened room, close your eyes, concentrate on your breathing, and relax into the wonder of present moment experience. Try it right now!

I'd also highlight the benefits of journaling and goal setting. This can help process emotions, foster gratitude, and stimulate free-flowing thoughts, all of which will make you happier.

Furthermore, I would love you to give mind mapping a go. This technique encourages three-dimensional thinking and the discovery of unexpected connections, stimulating creative thinking and idea generation.

Lastly, I'd like you to set goals right now! Make the goals realistic and measurable.
- By this time next week, I will have …
- By this time next month, I will be able to …
- By this time in three months, I will have …
- By this time next year, I will have succeeded in …

# Laura Ingalls Wilder

Laura Ingalls Wilder was born on February 7, 1867, in Pepin, Wisconsin, USA.

Before she found her calling as a writer, Laura Ingalls Wilder led a life rich with experiences that would later serve as the inspiration for her books. Growing up in a pioneer family, she experienced hardships and adventures on the American frontier. Her family's constant movement to different territories exposed her to a diverse range of landscapes and cultures.

After marrying Almanzo Wilder in 1885, Laura Ingalls Wilder embraced the role of a farmer's wife and mother, raising their daughter Rose. Despite the demands of daily life and the challenges of farming, Wilder would often share her childhood memories and family anecdotes with her daughter, sparking a desire to write down her experiences.

It wasn't until her 60s, however, that Laura Ingalls Wilder finally became a published author. Encouraged by her daughter Rose, who had become a successful writer herself, Wilder began recording her memories.

In 1932, at the age of 65, Laura Ingalls Wilder published her first book, *Little House in the Big Woods*. The novel, based on her early childhood in Wisconsin, enchanted readers with its portrayal of pioneer life of a bygone era. The book was an immediate success and paved the way for a series of beloved novels that would chronicle Wilder's life from her childhood through her marriage and beyond.

Wilder's literary journey continued with the publication of subsequent books in the series, including *Little House on the Prairie* and *These Happy Golden Years*.

Laura Ingalls Wilder's journey inspires aspiring writers to follow their dreams and pursue their passions, regardless of age or perceived limitations.

# Step four: Unleash creativity!

Creativity isn't about having a ridiculous talent for art or music to show off to the world. Creativity is for everybody. The more creative you are, the happier you will be both personally and professionally.

When I first got the idea of writing this book, I immediately thought of my creative pastimes: music, writing, design, photography, etc. These are all pretty obvious choices. However, you'll be amazed at what else is out there. I've done a bit of research into some of the ways we can indulge our creativity and I've tried to find some organizations that'll help you along the way. I have also listed some practical ways you can seek out other people and groups to collaborate with and help you along your creative journey. There are also prompts and challenges designed to whet your creative appetite.

You may already know the area of creativity that you wish to be involved with. But, as we have already discussed in this booklet, creativity knows no boundaries. Creative artistic fields are blurred at the edges; one discipline runs into others.

You don't have to do all of them. If you're not completely interested in one section then move onto the next.

Hopefully, there will be something here that resonates with you. Creativity is about taking something that is inside of you and putting it outside. Creativity is personal. So pick something that feels right for you.

**I can't promise that the information given in any of these links will be 100% accurate or that all of the groups will still be active.** I wanted to make this book as practical as possible. **I also apologize in advance that the links to organizations and information in this book are usually based in the USA and are Western.** A significant proportion of readers of this book will be based in North America and Western. But I really wish this book to be for everybody no matter where they are. I'm not American and I don't live in the West.

## Writing: Creative writing

Creative writing is extraordinary and transformative. It allows us to share our thoughts and experiences. Creative writing not only nurtures creativity but also improves critical thinking skills, helps us develop our voice, and engages us with the world.

We may wonder if people are lying when they say they love writing. We are taught to write at school. And, for me, being a cack-handed lefty, that was a painful experience. I was forever smudging the ink across the page. And yet, I do really love writing now; although I'm not sure why sometimes. But there is something pleasurable in crafting a sentence that you implicitly know is quite good. If you write a lot, it will help you communicate complex ideas more clearly. This will help you with people skills and relationships. It's a life skill and I'm incredibly grateful that I started blogging and writing books.

There's nothing worse than "writers' block". But, there's less reason to suffer "writers' block" these days. There are more and more tools online to help you with your creative writing. Engaging with writing prompts can spark storytelling and creative writing. I will talk about Artificial Intelligence elsewhere in this book. AI chatbots like ChatGPT are brilliant at coming up with prompts. And, because ChatGPT is a chatbot, you can chat with it. Explain the context of your creative story and ask it to list ten ideas of "what happened next". This is better than getting random prompts online without any context.

Refer back to the mind mapping section where you will find a few challenges that connect mind mapping to creative writing.

**Character exploration**: Create a detailed character profile for a fictional character. Then, write a short story or scene featuring that character, referring to parts of their back story you fleshed out in the character profile.

**Time travel tale**: Imagine you have the ability to travel through time. Write a short story about someone who discovers this power and their adventures in different time periods.

**Dialogue focus**: Write a conversation between two characters without any dialogue tags or descriptions. Challenge yourself to convey the emotions, intentions, and dynamics of the characters solely through dialogue.

**Flash fiction**: Write a complete story in less than 500 words. You may like to put a time limit on the first draft, maybe one hour. This challenge encourages concise storytelling and the ability to capture a compelling narrative in a short format.

**Writing from different perspectives**: Choose a familiar story or fairy tale and rewrite it from a different character's perspective. Explore the motivations, thoughts, and emotions of a secondary character and reimagine the events through their eyes.

**Genre mash-up**: Combine two different genres that you enjoy and create a unique story that blends their elements. For example, mix elements of science fiction and romance or mystery and fantasy. Explore the possibilities and create an engaging narrative.

- ChatGPT https://chat.openai.com/
- 25 Creative Writing Prompts for your Writing Group | Lake Seminole Square https://lakeseminoleseniorliving.com/blog/creative-writing-prompts/
- The Write Life Community | Facebook https://www.facebook.com/groups/TheWriteLifeGroup/
- Inked Voices | Peer Writing Groups https://www.inkedvoices.com/group/writing_groups/

- 11 Top Writing Communities You Should Join and Why https://nybookeditors.com/2015/11/11-top-writing-communities-you-should-join-and-why/
- Writing groups | Meetup https://www.meetup.com/topics/writing/
- Creative Writing groups in USA | Meetup https://www.meetup.com/topics/creative-writing/us/

## Writing: Journalism

Journalism isn't just a profession. With the rise of Web 2.0, we now have citizen journalists who are amateur enthusiasts with particular interests who can reach audiences that traditional news outlets do not. Journalists get a bad rap these days. They are blamed for misinformation caused by the changes in technology and yet more and more of them are being thrown in prisons and murdered each year. So, far from spreading misinformation, some journalists are publishing news that powerful people don't want published. So, I for one am grateful for these brave people.

- 10 must-join Facebook groups for journalists https://www.journalism.co.uk/news/10-facebook-groups-for-journalists-to-join/s2/a740420/
- JOURNALISM | Facebook https://www.facebook.com/groups/Journalistism/
- Online Journalism groups | Meetup https://www.meetup.com/topics/online-journalism/
- How Journaling Can Help You in Hard Times

https://greatergood.berkeley.edu/article/item/how_journaling_can_help_you_in_hard_times

## Writing: Non-fiction

Non-fiction writing is no less creative than creative writing. It allows you to crystallize your thoughts and affect other humans with them. Non-fiction has the power to inform, educate, and provoke. Non-fiction writing encourages critical thinking, research skills, and the ability to present facts in a compelling and engaging manner. These are indispensable and marketable skills in today's AI-enhanced world.

I have written eight non-fiction books and so I can testify as to its importance. Writing and publishing a non-fiction book, rightly or wrongly, elevates you to the level of "expert" in the eyes of many.

Pretty much anyone can publish an ebook, paperback book and audiobook on Amazon. When I learned how easy this was back in 2012, I immediately started writing books. Publishing books benefited me by getting my name (and personal brand) out there. People saw that I'd written a book about a subject and so they were more likely to contact me for business as a result.

Writing books also helped my self confidence. I'll never forget teachers telling me how appallingly bad my English spelling, grammar, and writing was. They were probably right. I probably was a bad student at school and some of the other kids were probably better than me. But, it's nice to think that I've written books that thousands of people have read after such an inauspicious start to my writing career.

Non-fiction books of only 15,000 words can be sold on Amazon. So, my advice to you now. Open a Google doc and start writing about what you know. There is more advice on how to write non-fiction books on my blog at Rob Cubbon https://robcubbon.com

If you are interested in developing your non-fiction writing, I would consider starting a blog or regularly posting your non-fiction writing to social media channels.

You can start by writing about what you know.

**How-to guide**: Choose a skill or hobby that you are knowledgeable about and write a step-by-step guide on it. Break down the process, offer practical tips, and provide clear instructions to help readers understand and follow along. Focus on readability.

**Personal essay**: Write a personal essay about a significant event or experience in your life. Reflect on the impact it had on you, what you learned from it, or how it shaped your perspective. Share your insights and emotions with honesty and depth.

**Opinion piece**: Share your thoughts and opinions on a current or controversial topic. Present a well-reasoned argument, back it up with evidence or personal experiences, and engage readers in a thoughtful discussion.

- Nonfiction Authors Association https://nonfictionauthorsassociation.com/
- Non Fiction Writers groups | Meetup https://www.meetup.com/topics/non-fiction-writers/
- Writers of Non-fiction | Facebook https://www.facebook.com/groups/217524621686329/
- PEN America https://pen.org/
- 22 Online Writing Groups on Facebook That Are Worth Your Time https://thewritelife.com/facebook-groups-for-writers/

## Writing: Poetry and the spoken word

Poetry, the rhythmic expression of emotions and ideas, is one of the hardest art forms to master. Capturing the essence of human experience and evoking emotions with only a few words is the poet's challenge. Engaging in poetry as a hobby opens the door to self-discovery, empathy, and the magic of language.

Writing a decent book is hard enough, but writing good poetry, for me, is one of the most difficult art forms to master. Sure, we can all write poems but, surely, there are few people in this world who can write good poems. And yet it's an art form that keeps coming into my consciousness. I gave up writing poetry when I was still a kid. As I write these words, I realize that I should give it another go. Suffice to say, I have huge respect for those people who craft art with words and get up on stage to recite them.

Exploring poetry writing or participating in spoken word events can be a cathartic and creative means of self-expression. It allows you to experiment with language, rhythm, and storytelling.

**Found poetry**: Take a book, newspaper article, or any written material and select or cut out random words or phrases. Rearrange these random words and phrases to create new sentences. Explore the unexpected connections and meanings that emerge from these found words and use them in a poem. This is how David Bowie wrote the lyrics to Moonage Daydream and other songs.

**Stream of consciousness**: Set a timer for a specific duration (e.g., 5 minutes) and write a poem without stopping or censoring your thoughts. Allow your stream of consciousness to flow onto the page. Don't worry about grammar or punctuation—just let your thoughts and feelings pour out.

**Emotional snapshot**: Capture a moment or an emotion in a snapshot. Write a short poem that conveys the essence of a moment or an emotion through sensory language. Focus on evoking feelings and creating a sensory experience for the reader.

**Poetic forms**: Challenge yourself to write a poem in a specific poetic form, such as a sonnet, haiku, villanelle, or pantoum. Follow the rules and structure of the form while expressing your thoughts and emotions.

- Spoken Word groups | Meetup https://www.meetup.com/topics/spoken-word/

## Art: General

The Arts is an all-encompassing term that includes painting, sketching, sculpture and a whole lot more.

Creating and enjoying art has surprising health benefits. Engaging in the creative process helps improve cognitive ability. Challenging yourself to learn new artistic techniques can potentially ward off Dementia. For older people, art can be used as an avenue for self-expression, stimulating the formation of new neural pathways in your brain, hence the potential to fend off neuro degenerative diseases.

Here are some general arts meetups and Facebook Groups.

- Art Talks | Facebook https://www.facebook.com/groups/132477014043792/
- Artalks | Facebook https://www.facebook.com/groups/artalk/
- Americans for the Arts https://www.americansforthearts.org/
- Art groups in USA | Meetup https://www.meetup.com/topics/art/us/

# Art: Sketching / drawing

Many of us haven't drawn anything by hand since childhood. But why should kids get all the fun? Sketching and drawing is a cheap creative release. It is only the fear of creating something bad that's holding you back. When you were a kid, other kids often laughed at you, but that didn't stop you from trying to draw something in art class.

So, buy some soft pencils and blank paper, or just grab some paper and pens that are lying around your house, sit by a window and try one of the following drawing prompts.

**Expressing emotions**: Close your eyes and think of an emotion or feeling. Try to translate that emotion into an abstract visual representation through sketching. Think about the lines, shapes, and shading techniques that will convey the emotion.

**Everyday objects**: Choose a common object around you, such as a coffee mug, a pair of shoes, or a houseplant. Sketch it from different angles or experiment with different styles, such as realistic, minimalistic, or abstract.

**Dreamy landscapes**: Imagine an ideal landscape that represents a place of tranquility or adventure for you. Sketch a picturesque scene with rolling hills, a serene beach, or a mystical forest. The good thing about sketching from imagination or doing abstracts is that no one can say "it doesn't look like that!"

**Something from outside**: Head outdoors and find a natural element like a leaf, a rock, or a tree bark. Bring it home, place it on a table near a window and try to recreate it on paper. Focus on capturing the textures and details through sketching, paying attention to the unique patterns and shapes.

**Yourself**: Hold up your hand and clench it into a fist. Can you sketch its likeness? Get a table mirror, and try to sketch your eye. A self portrait may be considered too much of a challenge at first but, what better way to get to know yourself?

## Art: Brass rubbing and rubbing in general

Brass rubbing was originally a largely British hobby of placing tracing paper over the brass plaques found in churches, and recording them by rubbing charcoal pencil over the paper, reproducing the imprint of the plaque's design.

However, you can create rubbings of anything such as textured walls, manhole covers, or rough tree bark. You may think that this type of drawing involves little creative input. But it's up to you to create a beautiful rubbing. And rubbings can be taken home, improved upon with charcoal, pencils, and paints, and turned into significant artworks.

**Abstract expressions**: You can combine different

materials and textures on one piece of paper. Overlay rubbings from various objects or textures to create visually intriguing patterns. Allow your imagination to guide the process.

**Personal artifacts**: Choose household objects, such as jewelry, sentimental items, or credit cards. Place them on a surface and use rubbing techniques to transfer their textures onto paper. You could do rubbings of the possessions of each member of your household or rubbings of items in each room.

**Outside rubbings**: Take a walk and collect leaves, tree bark, or interesting textures you come across. Use rubbing techniques to transfer the textures onto paper. Experiment with different pressure and materials to capture the different patterns.

# Art: Mood boarding

Mood boarding is a creative process that involves visually capturing the essence of a theme. It can consist of a blank piece of card that you can glue magazine cut-outs on to; or it can consist of a board where pieces of paper and fabric can be pinned; or you can make digital mood boards, most notably on Canva https://canva.com.

The purpose of mood boarding is to create a visual representation of a specific mood, style, or atmosphere. By curating a collection of visuals, mood boarding serves as a powerful tool for creative exploration and visual storytelling. Mood boards should be placed in an area of your home you frequently see. If the mood board is digital, consider putting it on your computer desktop or on your phone. The purpose of frequently seeing a mood board is to allow the theme to seep into your subconscious so that its meaning resonates deeply with you. This is especially true if the mood board represents your aspirations, like your ideal future life.

**Creative Project**: Create a mood board to kickstart a creative project, such as writing a book, designing a website, or launching a new product. This can be done either on your own or if the project is a collaboration. Starting a new project can be daunting but a mood board can be a great starting point. Compile visual references, color schemes, typography, and imagery that align with the project's theme and desired outcome.

**Travel destination**: Create a mood board that captures the essence and mood of a dream travel destination. Gather images, colors, textures, and typography that evoke the feeling of that specific place.

**Home interiors**: Curate a mood board that represents your ideal home. Gather images of furniture, color palettes, textures, and decorative elements that align with your desired ambiance and style. Explore different themes, such as minimalist, bohemian, or Scandinavian, and play with various design elements.

**Brand identity**: Develop a mood board that showcases the visual identity of a fictional or real brand. Collect images, fonts, logos, and color palettes that convey the brand. This will help you in all areas of design and art.

**Inspirational quotes**: Create a mood board that combines inspiring quotes with visually appealing designs. Select meaningful quotes that resonate with you and pair them with complementary imagery, typography, and colors.

**Dream goals**: Design a mood board that represents your dreams, aspirations, and goals. Combine images, symbols, and motivational quotes that inspire you and reflect your vision for the future. Use colors and visuals that evoke a sense of excitement, motivation, and possibility.

# Art: Painting and drawing

How do you make something cheerful using only dark colors? How do you make a finger look more realistic? If you accidentally put the wrong color in the wrong part of the picture, what do you do about it?

Problem-solving is front and center in painting and drawing more so than in other creative processes. By painting, you can improve your creative mind while also developing critical-thinking abilities. And this is good for combating or warding off generative diseases.

Painting and drawing also helps you develop fine motor skills. These motor skills are developed by using tiny muscles in your hands and wrists to make small but precise movements. This is important for young children as well as adults.

The University of St. Augustine theorizes that visual arts (like painting) helps older adults maintain and even improve their fine motor skills. Every time you use a paintbrush or a pencil, you're building muscle and neural connections that are crucial for other day-to-day activities.

- Painting and Fine Arts Group | Facebook https://www.facebook.com/groups/208173569849985/
- Painting groups | Meetup https://www.meetup.com/topics/painting/
- Drawing groups in USA | Meetup https://www.meetup.com/en-AU/topics/draw/us/
- Learning to Draw groups in USA | Meetup https://www.meetup.com/en-AU/topics/learn-to-draw/us/
- Drawbox | A Free, exercise based approach to learning the fundamentals of drawing https://drawabox.com/

## Art: Sculpture

Sculpting can claim many of the previously mentioned physical and mental benefits of other creative pastimes. However, sculpting is also inherently fun and playful. Most of us will think of art lessons at school where we got our hands dirty playing around with clay and the teacher getting angry.

Adults can benefit mentally from exploring the

same sense of playfulness that they had during their childhood and without supervision. Sculpting provides a unique opportunity to do this.

Working with clay or other sculpting materials allows you to shape and mold your ideas into reality. Sculpting and pottery provide a hands-on creative experience, enabling people to explore different textures, forms, and techniques. It offers a chance to engage in a three-dimensional art space that photography, painting, and drawing can't.

- Ohio Outdoor Sculpture http://oos.sculpturecenter.org/
- Sculptors | Facebook https://www.facebook.com/groups/488468501598251/
- SCULPTORS groups | Meetup https://www.meetup.com/topics/sculptors/
- National Sculpture Society https://nationalsculpture.org/

## Art: Sculptural pottery

Taking pottery to a sculptural level involves creating three-dimensional forms and sculptures using clay. It allows individuals to explore texture, form, and expressiveness in their ceramic creations.

- The American Ceramic Society | For Ceramics and Glass Professionals https://ceramics.org/

- Ceramics and sculpture - Melville Community Arts Association https://melvillearts.com.au/class_category/ceramics-and-sculpture/

## Art: Community art projects

Collaborating in community-based art projects, such as murals, public sculptures, or art installations, provides an opportunity to contribute to the local community and engage with others creatively. You can get in touch with your local government to see if there are any community art projects in your area. What better way would there be to meet people than if you are actively trying to make your shared public spaces more beautiful?

- Art groups | Meetup https://www.meetup.com/topics/art/
- Association for Public Art https://www.associationforpublicart.org/what-we-do/

## Art: Mosaic art and collage

There are two parts to creating mosaic art. It firstly involves assembling small pieces of glass, tile, or other materials from discarded industrial waste or from ordinary household items. And, secondly, these materials are positioned or glued together to form intricate patterns or images. It allows individuals to explore color, texture, and composition whilst creating stunning visual artwork.

**Magazine mash-up**: Gather a stack of old magazines or newspapers and flip through them to find interesting images, patterns, and textures. Cut out the elements that catch your eye. You can either cut around the shapes in the images or get creative with the scissors and cut your own shapes from attractive textual backgrounds. Finally, combine them in a collage to create your own unique artwork.

**Found object mosaic**: Collect small, everyday objects like buttons, beads, seashells, or even broken ceramics. Create a mosaic artwork using these found objects, arranging and gluing them onto a surface to form a unique composition.

**Color palette challenge**: Gather together some old magazines, choose a limited color palette of 3-5 colors and create a mosaic artwork using only those colors. Experiment with different shades, textures, and shapes within the chosen palette to create depth and visual interest.

**Wordplay collage**: Select a word or phrase and create a collage that represents or interprets its meaning. Use cut-out letters, words, or symbols from magazines or create your own with different materials like colored paper or fabric.

**Story collage**: Choose a favorite story, true or fictitious, or song lyrics and create a collage that illustrates or captures the essence of the narrative. This could be a news event, a nursery rhyme, or the plot

of a famous movie. Experiment with layering images, textures, and colors to convey the emotions or themes of the chosen piece.
- Mosaic Art groups | Meetup https://www.meetup.com/topics/mosaic-art/

## Art: Collage and mixed media art

Very similar to mosaic art, collage art involves combining various materials, such as magazine cut-outs, fabric, and found objects, to create visually engaging compositions. Mixed media art allows for the fusion of different artistic mediums, such as painting, drawing, and collage, in a single artwork.
- Mixed Media Art groups | Meetup https://www.meetup.com/topics/mixed-media-art/

## Art: Digital mosaic art or montage

Mosaic art can be created digitally. You have the usual choice of image editors: expensive (Adobe Photoshop), cheap (Affinity Photo) and free (GIMP). You can gather images and backgrounds from the web to create your own mosaic (or maybe you would call it a collage or a montage).

**Personal symbolism**: Explore your personal symbolism and create a mosaic artwork that represents your personality. Choose symbols from the Internet that have personal meaning to you or images from your own photographic archive and incorporate them into your mosaic design. Get images of you when you were younger, your hometown, or the places you visited that were important to you. Create an artwork whilst embarking on a voyage of self-discovery.

**Cultural fusion**: Pick two cultures, your own and one familiar to you. Explore these cultures' images online. Notice the differences and create a mosaic artwork that combines elements from the two artistic traditions. Fuse together patterns, motifs, or techniques from different cultures to create a visually rich piece of digital art.

## Art: Comic book creation

For those interested in storytelling and illustration, creating a comic book can be a fun and creative endeavor. You can develop characters, plotlines, and artwork to craft your unique comic book narratives. This is yet another discipline that could be enhanced with the help of Artificial Intelligence (AI). AI image generators are really good at creating comic book characters and backgrounds in particular styles. And AI chatbots, such as ChatGPT, are really good at coming up with story prompts to help you develop your comic's plots and storylines.

## Photography

We all have a phone with a great camera and we've all taken some great photos. Photography as a hobby or art form has possibly the lowest barrier to entry. I used to wander the streets of Paris and London with a heavy bag with a dSLR with black and white film, with multiple lenses and a tripod. (That last sentence sounded hopelessly old-fashioned). Like countless others, I love to experiment with photography.

Photography offers endless opportunities for personal growth and learning. You can delve into the technical aspects of photography, such as composition, lighting, and post-processing, and develop new skills and a deeper understanding of the art form. You will become more attuned to your creative intuition.

And, for me, there are two creative processes to taking a photograph. There's the process of taking the shot and then the process of editing or enhancing the image once it's been taken. I enjoy both. There's a great amount of information online about how to take better photographs. And with photography, as with every creative endeavor, it's best to explore the medium with other people. So here are some links to help you find supportive photography communities.

**Color exploration**: For any given day, choose a specific color and challenge yourself to capture a series of photographs that predominantly feature that color. This particular challenge is only good for a few days. You could also create mood boards of your old photographs where the only connecting theme is color. You could use Photoshop or another image editor to change the hue of the images so the selected color appears more similar.

**Everyday beauty**: Challenge yourself to find beauty in everyday objects or scenes. Take a walk around your home and take photographs that showcase the beauty in simplicity, such as a leaf on a sidewalk or the play of light or shadows on a wall.

**Perspective play**: Get down low, climb up high, or find unique angles to photograph familiar subjects or scenes. This can offer a unique perspective. In these days of Instagram, it's no longer such a strange thing to be seen going to extreme lengths to get the perfect shot. Just make sure you don't get arrested for suspected burglary.

**Reflections**: Look for opportunities to capture interesting reflections in windows, water bodies, or shiny surfaces. Experiment with composition and angles to create visually striking images that play with reflections and their relationship to the surroundings.

**Minimalism**: Embrace the concept of minimalism in your photography. Seek out minimalistic compositions with clean lines, simplicity, and negative space. Capture images that convey a sense of calmness and simplicity. Minimalist photography puts composition to the fore.

- 11 of the Best Facebook Groups for Photographers https://www.format.com/magazine/resources/photography/best-facebook-groups-for-photographer-networking

- Top 25 Online Photography Communities and Forums 2023 https://www.pixpa.com/blog/online-photography-communities-to-follow
- I LOVE PHOTOGRAPHY | Facebook https://www.facebook.com/groups/569453210073902/

## Graphic design and digital art

Following on from photography is digital art. I have experienced great joy by enhancing and editing my own photography with Photoshop. But now Artificial Intelligence is creating a whole new suite of tools whereby we can enhance and improve images with text prompts of spoken words. There are new AI tools being released every day, which makes this area difficult to quantify. A lot of the new tools are beta versions and are free for general use so, now, creating your own professional digital art is just a Google search away.

Aside from editing and enhancing your own photography, Artificial Intelligence can now create new images. I have been using different AI image generators for many months now. My favorite is Midjourney but there are many others, including Leonardo, Stable Diffusion, DALL·E 2, for example. You may think that just asking a computer to make an image for you isn't that creative. But, as I argue in this book, Artificial Intelligence can enhance our creativity and force us to be even more creative and to think even further outside the box. I often marry two different Midjourney images together in Photoshop to create something new.

We also have to get into specifics of design applications in order to engage with this particular discipline. Don't assume the best results will only come from the expensive Adobe Creative Cloud. There are many mid priced options you can explore, such as Affinity Photo ($70) which is similar to Photoshop. There are also free, open source options such as GIMP and the online design tool, Canva, which has both free and paid subscriptions.

Exploring digital tools and software for graphic design and digital art can open up new creative possibilities. People can experiment with digital illustration, typography, photo manipulation, or even create digital collages. This medium offers versatility, accessibility, and, with the aid of Artificial Intelligence, you have a platform to bring your imaginative ideas to life.

Creating art with these tools is not only satisfying but will also teach you how to design and problem-solving skills.

**Digital illustration**: Choose a subject and create a digital illustration using digital brushes, shapes, and layers. Experiment with different styles and techniques to bring your illustration to life. You can use Affinity Designer ($70), which is an Adobe Illustrator equivalent and is free for the first month. You could also use the free, open source, Inkscape.

**Typography exploration**: Choose a word or a phrase and experiment with different typography styles, layouts, and treatments to create a visually appealing typographic composition.

**Poster design**: Create a poster for an event, movie, or a cause. Experiment with composition, typography, colors, and imagery to capture attention and effectively communicate the intended message.

## Film and video production

Yet another creative avenue where the barrier to entry has been recently reduced massively due to new technology. You used to have to spend ages setting up a scene, waiting for the correct time of day for the light, while mounting expensive and heavy cameras on tripods or on tracks. Now, anyone can point their phone at anything and make something that looks and sounds good. If you don't agree with me now, just wait to see what happens next year.

I'm amazed at what technology can do in these particular creative fields. But, just because technology has reduced the complexity of the discipline doesn't mean that it'll reduce *your* creativity. Indeed, your creativity can be enhanced.

Filmmaking and video production is a creative outlet for storytelling and visual expression. You can now create short films, documentaries, or just present your personal videos with your own creative touch.

- Film and Video Production groups | Meetup https://www.meetup.com/topics/film-and-video-production/

## Music: General

Sometimes, music can seem to have an extremely high barrier to entry. Especially if you regularly go to watch other musicians play, as I do. Sometimes the levels of expertise of others can be discouraging. Sometimes, other guitarists make me want to go home and burn all my guitars. But, as we all know, music can elevate your mood and heal your pain.

And here are some links to groups where you can meet and network with other musicians. And, remember, the best musicians will encourage you and elevate your abilities. You will improve your technique faster by playing with musicians who are "superior" to you than you would by playing on your own.

Here are some Meetup and Facebook groups.

- Music groups in USA | Meetup https://www.meetup.com/topics/music/us/
- Love Local Music with US | Facebook https://www.facebook.com/groups/210341205729667/
- USA MUSICIAN NETWORKING | Facebook https://www.facebook.com/groups/236287586541089/
- Music Sharing Network (MSN) | Facebook https://www.facebook.com/groups/1946177372306874

## Music: Playing instruments

Playing a musical instrument as a hobby offers personal development, cognitive enhancement, emotional well-being, and a sense of community. The act of playing an instrument taps into our creativity and allows us to connect with ourselves and others in a profound way.

Learning an instrument can improve your concentration and cognition. According to a study of twins, including one who played an instrument and one who didn't, learning an instrument can reduce your risk of developing Alzheimer's later in life by a third.

**Daily practice challenge**: This is where you set a specific amount of time each day for a certain challenge. For example, playing different scales and arpeggios up and down the fretboard. This is a healthy alternative to playing every day without any focus. You will get better quicker by using this method.

**Technique focus**: Choose a specific technique or skill that you want to improve on your instrument. For me with the guitar, there are a few obvious choices. It could be an alternative picking method, "the claw" finger picking method, finger dexterity, bending notes, or, dare I say it, learning scales and playing them incessantly. This is a nasty, boring and uncreative way to do things. But, if you devote dedicated practice sessions to honing a particular skill, you will most definitely improve.

**Collaborative performance**: Collaborate with other musicians or friends who play different instruments.

**Genre exploration**: Step outside your comfort zone and explore a genre of music that is different from what you usually play. Learn a song or an instrumental piece that represents that genre.

**Improvisation challenges**: Set aside dedicated practice time for improvisation. Create simple backing tracks or use existing ones from YouTube, and challenge yourself to improvise melodies or solos over them. This will help develop your musical ear, phrasing, and expression.

**Recording session**: Create a simple recording setup or find a recording studio and challenge yourself to record and produce a short musical piece or composition. This encourages creativity, attention to detail, and will help you understand the recording process.

Here are some Meetup groups for those who are learning instruments or for those who want to learn an instrument.

- Learning to play a musical instrument groups | Meetup https://www.meetup.com/topics/learning-to-play-a-musical-instrument/

# Music: Singing

Singing is a remarkable and universal form of self-expression that brings joy, emotional release, and other benefits. It serves as a natural stress reliever, releasing endorphins and promoting a sense of well-being. Additionally, singing is a powerful way to build connections, whether through group performances, karaoke nights, or online collaborations.

**Vocal warm-up routine:** Develop a consistent vocal warm-up routine to prepare your voice before singing. These can be scales or holding notes for as long as possible. This will improve breath control, vocal range, resonance, and articulation.

**Song interpretation:** Choose a favorite song and challenge yourself to interpret it in a unique way. Experiment with different vocal styles, genres, phrasing, and emotional expressions to make the song your own.

**Vocal harmony experimentation:** Challenge yourself to learn and sing vocal harmonies to recorded melodies or with a friend. Explore different harmonization techniques such as thirds, fifths, etc. This helps develop your ear and enhances your ability to hit correct notes.

**Acapella challenge:** Select a song and challenge yourself to sing it acapella, without any instrumental accompaniment. This exercise helps develop your sense of pitch, rhythm, and phrasing.

**Vocal range expansion:** Work on expanding your

vocal range by practicing exercises that target higher or lower notes. Explore different vocal registers (chest voice, head voice, falsetto) and practice exercises that gradually push your range boundaries.

**Songwriting and composition**: Challenge yourself to write an original song. This is one of the most fulfilling creative exercises. It challenges you in many ways as you need to evoke meaning by combining melody, rhythm, and lyrics. This allows for creative expression and helps you develop a unique musical identity.

## Music: Singing in choirs

Singing actually brings additional health benefits over simply listening or playing music. Studies have shown that singing enhances your breathing, posture, and even helps with muscle tension. Singing in a choir can synchronize your heartbeat. This happens because choir members tend to breathe together, causing their hearts to beat together. Research has also demonstrated that melodies influence heart rates, causing the pulses of the singers to rise and fall together when singing in a group.

In 2012, researchers in Cardiff University in Wales uncovered evidence that lung cancer patients who sang in choirs had greater expiratory capacity than people who did not. Other than these health benefits particular to choral singing, choristers will enjoy other health benefits of music, including: the social bonding of being together in a large group engaged in a positive activity, the cognitive stimulation of having to memorize their parts, the reduced stress levels, the basic therapeutic nature of music in itself, etc.

Have you ever been to a choir practice? It's usually a gathering of very happy people.

Here are some links for online groups that will connect you with choirs in your area.
- Choir lovers and choral composition | Facebook https://www.facebook.com/groups/2228835682/
- One Day One Choir - RSA https://www.thersa.org/blog/2018/08/one-day-one-choir
- Community Sings | Chorus America https://chorusamerica.org/singers/community-sings

## Cooking and recipe creation

Get creative when you're getting hungry. Beyond mere sustenance, this art form allows you to express your unique tastes and preferences. Exploring new ingredients, experimenting with techniques, and crafting original recipes stimulates the senses, nourishes the body, and brings people together. It encourages culinary innovation, cultural appreciation, and a deeper understanding of the diverse tapestry of food. It's great to play around with ingredients, flavors, and cooking techniques.

I always like to get the meal to look nice on the dish. Tie this creative pastime in with photography and take an image of each meal you cook. Try new recipes, modify existing ones, or even create your own unique dishes. You can use the AI chatbot ChatGPT to suggest ingredients, recipes, and flavors. Provide the chatbot with the contents of your fridge and ask it to come up with ideas for your next culinary masterpiece.

It goes without saying that you can share your creations online and off. People will enjoy your recipes on social media and even more in real life, as no one will say no to a good meal.

This process allows for self-expression, innovation, and the satisfaction of enjoying a delicious meal.

**Ingredient exploration**: Choose an ingredient that you enjoy or have on hand. Create a recipe that highlights and celebrates that ingredient as the star. Experiment with different cooking methods, flavor combinations, and techniques to showcase its versatility.

**DIY condiments or sauces**: Develop a recipe for a homemade condiment, sauce, or dressing. Experiment with different combinations of herbs, spices, and ingredients to create a flavor profile that complements various dishes.

**Fusion cuisine**: Combine two different cuisines or culinary traditions to create a unique fusion recipe, for example, Italian and Thai. Explore each cuisine's flavors, ingredients, and cooking techniques and find creative ways to blend them.

**Get the colors right**: Concentrate on creating

dishes that look as good as they taste. Carefully select vegetables and other ingredients based on their color and esthetic qualities and then arrange them together on the dish to form a composition that is pleasing to the eye. Combine this with photography and share these dishes and their recipes on social media.

## Dance and movement

Express your soul creatively with your whole body. Dance and movement transcends words to communicate emotions, stories, and cultural expressions. As a hobby, dance allows individuals to connect with their bodies, emotions, and the world around them.

Engaging in dance or other forms of movement-based activities can foster creativity through bodily expression. Dance is a way for people of all ages to stay fit and can improve your muscle tone, strength, and endurance. You could explore different dance styles, create your own choreography, or even participate in improvisational dance. Dance provides a unique way to connect with emotions, connect with people, and experience the joy of physical expression.

**Partner dance connection**: If you have a dance partner, explore the art of partner dancing. Challenge yourselves to create a seamless and connected dance routine that requires trust, synchronization, and mutual understanding of movement.

**Improvisation exploration**: Set aside a dedicated time for improvisation. Allow yourself to move freely and spontaneously without predefined choreography. Embrace the moment and let your body respond to the music, emotions, and environment.

**Everyday object movement**: Select a random everyday object, such as a chair, a hat, or a scarf, and incorporate it into your dance routine. Experiment with using the object as a prop or as an extension of your body, incorporating it into your movements in creative ways.

- Dance and Movement groups | Meetup https://www.meetup.com/topics/dance-and-movement/
- Dance/Movement Therapy Community Group - ON PAUSE | Facebook https://www.facebook.com/groups/AmericanDanceTherapyAssociation/

## Interior design and home décor

The spaces in our homes are the stage for important moments in our lives. It's therefore beneficial that your personal spaces provide comfort, support, and positive energy.

Interior design and home décor have the power to transform living spaces into personalized sanctuaries, reflecting our unique tastes and personalities. By embracing interior design, you can not only enhance your living spaces but also create a haven that nurtures well-being and reflects your personal aesthetic vision.

Redesigning and decorating living spaces can be a creative and collaborative project with family members. You can experiment with colors, furniture arrangements, and decorative elements to create personalized and visually pleasing environments.

**Room transformation**: Choose a room in your home and challenge yourself to redesign and transform it. Create a mood board or collage to gather inspiration, explore different color schemes, furniture arrangements, lighting options, and decorative elements to create a cohesive and inviting space.

**Small space solutions**: Focus on optimizing and maximizing the functionality and aesthetics of a small or challenging space, such as a studio apartment or a compact room. Explore clever storage solutions, multifunctional furniture, and creative layout designs to make the most of the available area.

**Statement wall or focal point**: Choose a wall or area in your home and create a striking focal point. Experiment with bold wallpapers, accent paint colors, gallery walls, or decorative features to make a statement and draw attention to that specific area.

**Mood-enhancing lighting**: Explore different lighting options and fixtures to create various moods and ambiance in different areas of your home. Experiment with task lighting, accent lighting, and dimmers.

- Interior Design & Decor | Facebook https://www.facebook.com/groups/interiordesignndecor/

- Home Decorating groups | Meetup https://www.meetup.com/topics/homedecorating/
- Home - The Inspired Room https://theinspiredroom.net/

## Gardening and landscaping

Gardening has positive effects on your mental and physical health. The pandemic forced people to stay indoors and some of us missed the opportunity to connect with nature in a creative way.

Creating beautiful outdoor spaces can be a creative and rewarding endeavor. If you do have access to a garden, you could design and plan it, select different plants and flowers, and arrange them in aesthetically pleasing ways.

- Gardening USA - Homesteading Self Sufficient Living https://www.facebook.com/groups/gardening.usa/
- Landscaping Groups | Meetup https://www.meetup.com/topics/landscaping/
- Societies, Clubs and Organizations - American Horticultural Society https://ahsgardening.org/gardening-resources/societies-clubs-organizations/

## DIY crafts and upcycling

Engaging in do-it-yourself (DIY) crafts and upcycling projects encourages resourcefulness and creativity. If you have or live near a lot of old trash, you can repurpose old items, such as furniture, clothing, or household objects, and transform them into something new and unique. You can gift these objects to local homeless charities who are desperate for free furniture. This allows for self-expression, environmental consciousness, and the satisfaction of creating functional and visually appealing pieces.

- Upcycle My Stuff https://upcyclemystuff.com/
- Upcycling Artisans Create Beauty from Discards https://craftindustryalliance.org/upcycling-artisans-create-beauty-from-discards/
- Crafts DIY & upcycling | Facebook https://www.facebook.com/groups/1595751924060007/
- Make It New: Upcycle, Repurpose and DIY Ideas for Sharing and Inspiring | Facebook https://www.facebook.com/groups/MakeItNew/
- Upcycled furniture #upcyclerevolution | Facebook https://www.facebook.com/groups/427881090739426
- Upcycleit Australia | Facebook https://www.facebook.com/groups/upcycleit.com.au
- Repurpose + Upcycle = Inspiration https://www.facebook.com/groups/391970100943912

# Improvisation and acting

Someone once described improvisation as the "threshold of anxiety." Before they took the stage, they had all the usual daily concerns: paying the bills, work, family, etc. Then, as soon as they took the stage, it all melted away, and they were fully in the moment.

Improvisation workshops or acting classes unlock spontaneity and self-expression. These activities offer opportunities to explore different characters, emotions, and scenarios, fostering creativity through storytelling, collaboration, and the ability to think on one's feet. People can start acting at any time. Amateur productions are always looking for people of any age or people from different backgrounds to fill specific roles.

- Improv groups | Meetup https://www.meetup.com/topics/improv/

## Fashion design and clothing styling

Creating unique fashion designs or experimenting with personal styles can be an artistic outlet. You can sketch clothing ideas, sew garments, or mix and match outfits to create distinctive looks.

Looking good can make you feel good. Wearing different colors can alter your mood. Fashion design allows for self-expression, exploration of color and fabric, and, for many people, the ability to craft a personal aesthetic is a big pull.

- FASHION INTEREST GROUP | Facebook https://www.facebook.com/groups/FashionInterestGroup/

## Upcycled fashion

You can transform old clothing or fabric into new pieces. This is both creative and sustainable. You can repurpose, alter, or embellish garments from charity shops or thrift stores to create unique and eco-friendly fashion statements. This offers you the chance to wear art you've created and to craft a personal aesthetic.

Up-Cycled Cloth Collective | Facebook https://www.facebook.com/groups/UpCycledClothCollective/

## Jewelry making

And still on the subject of crafting a personal aesthetic, designing and crafting jewelry allows you to create wearable art. You can work with various materials, such as beads, wire, or metals, to make unique pieces that reflect your personal style.

- Jewelry Making groups | Meetup https://www.meetup.com/topics/jewelry/
- Jewelry Making Techniques groups | Meetup https://www.meetup.com/topics/jewelry-making-techniques/
- Jewelry Makers Learning Center | Facebook https://www.facebook.com/groups/113836439327040/
- Jewelry Classes | Bay Area Jewelry Making Class | The Crucible https://www.thecrucible.org/departments/jewelry/

## Woodworking and Carpentry

Working with wood allows you to create functional and visually appealing items. You could engage with woodworking projects, such as building furniture, crafting small wooden objects, or even carving intricate designs. Woodworking promotes craftsmanship, problem-solving, increased math abilities (when measuring), and the joy of working with natural materials.

- Carpentry groups | Meetup https://www.meetup.com/topics/carpentry/
- Woodworking Network (@WoodworkingBiz) / Twitter https://twitter.com/WoodworkingBiz
- Popular Woodworking | Woodworking advice, plans, projects, and plans https://www.popularwoodworking.com/

## Calligraphy and hand lettering

Another calming and artistic pursuit is calligraphy or hand lettering. You can learn different lettering styles, experiment with various writing tools, and create beautiful artworks to use as invitations, business cards or decorations.

- Calligraphy and Hand Lettering groups in USA | Meetup https://www.meetup.com/topics/calligraphy-and-hand-lettering/us/
- How To Do Modern Calligraphy (3 Popular Styles

2023) | Lettering Daily https://www.lettering-daily.com/modern-calligraphy/

## Candle making

Crafting candles allows individuals to experiment with different scents, colors, and shapes. It offers a sensory and artistic experience, and the end result can be used practically in your own home or given as thoughtful gifts.

- Candle Making groups | Meetup https://www.meetup.com/topics/candlemaking/
- Candles Are Us | Facebook https://www.facebook.com/groups/1413373205391631/
- Welcome to our Candle Making Group - Candle Making by Candle Makers https://candlemakingbycandlemakers.wordpress.com/about/

## Paper crafts

Paper crafts encompass a wide range of creative activities, including origami, paper cutting, and paper quilling. These crafts allow individuals to transform paper into intricate and visually appealing designs.

- Paper Crafts groups | Meetup https://www.meetup.com/topics/paper-crafts/
- Craft Warehouse Paper Crafts Group | Facebook https://www.facebook.com/groups/1571615619630224/

- Adriana's Paper Crafts Group https://adrianaspapercrafts.com/pages/adrianas-paper-crafts-group

## Puppetry and storytelling

Creating puppets and engaging in puppetry performances can tap into your imagination and storytelling skills. It offers a playful and interactive way to bring stories and characters to life.

- Puppeteers of America https://www.puppeteers.org/

These are just **some of the ways you can be creative**. Remember, creativity knows no boundaries. It's possible to be a great musician, writer, and artist at the same time. Don't pigeonhole yourself! Again, I would like to apologize if some of the links and the information I shared had a North American geographical bias. This is because I suspect most of the readers of this booklet will be from that part of the world. But, I'm not American and I don't live there or in Europe, so I'm aware that creativity is universal and I wish I could make this book more inclusive but practicalities render that impossible.

Another of the themes of this book is that creativity has to be a joint venture. Whatever your chosen creative discipline, you should try to collaborate with others. In the rest of this chapter, I will highlight some of **the ways you can find others to collaborate with in artistic endeavors.**

## Local art groups and organizations

A great way to connect with like-minded artists and find potential collaborators would be to seek out local art groups, associations, or organizations. Attend art exhibitions, workshops, or networking events organized by these groups to meet individuals who share similar artistic interests.

An obvious example of artistic networking from a musician's perspective is to go along to any "open mic" event. An "open mic" event is where musicians gather to perform a few songs each. They are fun and social activities. But they are also places where musicians meet other musicians who can then go on to collaborate. Just imagine a world if Lennon hadn't met McCartney, or Rodgers hadn't met Hammerstein, or Leiber hadn't met Stoller.

## Online artist communities and forums

Explore online platforms and forums dedicated to artists. For the digital artist, you have platforms such as DeviantArt, Behance, or ArtStation. These platforms provide opportunities to connect with artists from around the world, showcase your work, and find potential collaborators for joint projects.

- Artist Forum https://www.artistforum.com/

## Social media networking

I hesitate to write this section because, well, we all know social media networking can be incredibly powerful. But, we also all know it can also be a terrible waste of time and occasionally present us with the worst excesses of human nature.

Having said that, social media platforms like Instagram, Facebook, or Twitter, if used correctly, will help you to connect with artists and creative communities. Follow relevant hashtags and engage with posts to discover artists who align with you artistically. You can direct message or comment on their work. Always be positive. Everybody loves compliments. Ask questions about their creativity. The more successful and talented the person is, the more helpful they will be. This can also open doors for potential collaborations.

- Social Networking groups in USA | Meetup https://www.meetup.com/topics/socialnetwork/us/

## Art schools and universities

Is there an art school or university near you? Maybe they have workshops or courses where you'll have the opportunity to meet fellow artists and build connections within the artistic community. Collaborative projects are often encouraged within educational environments, providing opportunities to work alongside other talented individuals.

## Artist residencies and retreats

This is a long shot, but you could try to apply for an artist residence or retreat. These programs bring together creatives from different backgrounds and regions. These events offer a supportive environment for collaboration, allowing artists to work together on projects and exchange ideas.

- Americans for the Arts https://www.americansforthearts.org/

## Arts grants and funding opportunities

Apply for arts grants or funding programs that support collaborative projects. These opportunities not only provide financial support but also connect artists with resources and networks that can lead to fruitful collaborations.

- National Endowment for Arts https://www.arts.gov/grants/grants-for-arts-projects/program-description

In this chapter, I tried to give some practical examples of ways you can be creative. I hope that one of the suggestions helped you in some way. I appreciate that this is a huge field and there may have been subjects that you skipped. But I was surprised that there were some fun, artistic endeavors that I'd not heard of. And I would love to try some of these out.

I also appreciate that not all of us have access to

funding or have the wherewithal to attend workshops or courses. I also appreciate that everyone lives in different areas with different creative opportunities, so it has been difficult writing this part of the book so that it is universal and inclusive for all people in all areas of creativity.

# Albert Einstein

Albert Einstein was born in Ulm, Germany, in 1879. He displayed remarkable intellectual curiosity from an early age. As a young physicist, Einstein was captivated by the mysteries of light, motion, and the nature of space and time.

In his pursuit of understanding, he embarked on a creative thought experiment that would forever change the course of modern physics. Einstein imagined himself riding on a beam of light, contemplating what he would see and experience. This imaginative leap led him to question the fundamental nature of time and space, challenging the long-held belief in absolute space and time proposed by Sir Isaac Newton.

Einstein's breakthrough came from his special theory of relativity, published in 1905. In this groundbreaking work, he postulated that the laws of physics are the same for all observers moving at constant speeds relative to each other. Moreover, he proposed that the speed of light in a vacuum is constant and is the ultimate speed limit in the universe.

Einstein's theory of relativity had profound implications for our understanding of time, space, energy, and gravity. It introduced the concept of spacetime, a unified framework in which both time and space are interconnected. The theory also provided a mathematical foundation for understanding the behavior of objects traveling at high speeds and the phenomenon of time dilation.

The practical applications and beneficial effects of Einstein's theory of relativity are far-reaching. For instance, it has contributed to the development of GPS systems, as the accurate measurement of time is crucial for satellite-based positioning. Additionally, the theory has been instrumental in advancing our understanding of the cosmos, explaining the behavior of black holes, gravitational waves, and the expanding universe.

Einstein's creativity revolutionized physics and left an indelible mark on scientific inquiry. His work reshaped our understanding of the fundamental laws governing the universe and opened up new avenues for exploration and discovery.

# Step five: Maintaining a creative lifestyle

Maintaining a creative lifestyle can be a challenge as we grow. Responsibilities pile up and our time becomes scarce. However, we must reclaim our creativity and weave it into the fabric of our daily lives.

In this chapter, we explore practices for nurturing and sustaining a creative lifestyle. We will delve into the power of mindfulness, the art of meditation, and the benefits they bring to the creative process. We will also uncover the transformative potential of keeping a creative journal as a tool for self-expression and inspiration.

Life is a canvas waiting to be painted with the colors of our imagination. By cultivating a creative mindset, we can tap into the wellspring of our inner light, bringing forth unique artistic expression.

We also discuss time management, continuous learning, seeking feedback, and self-evaluation. By incorporating these practices into our lives, we can reignite the flame of creativity. We will learn to infuse our daily routines with moments of mindfulness, harness the power of meditation to enhance our creative focus, and document our journeys through the pages of a creative journal.

## Set aside time for creativity

Remember, we're creative types so we don't respond well to routines. But, as creatives, we should try to add at least some discipline into our lives. However, "setting aside time for creativity" is a bit of a contradiction in terms. Song writing, for example, is not something you can just start doing like making a cup of tea. Songs, like ideas, come to you out of nothing. You can go through some amazingly prolific periods when it all comes easily. You will also go through times when you get no inspiration and, sadly, no output. There's nothing worse than hitting a creative block. But, when you do, it'll feel like nothing can be done about it.

But, let's start with writing. If you are a writer, and I would seriously advise anyone to write a book, there's an obvious goal you can set yourself. Affirm that you will write x amount of words a day.

This is how I've written all of my books. It's absolutely perfect. It gamifies creativity. Remember, being creative is similar to playing when you were a kid. And, just like a kid, I get competitive with myself each day to see if I can reach or exceed my target. This goal puts light at the end of the tunnel and gives you milestones to get there. "Great, I've written 7,000 words already, if I keep this up, I'll nearly be halfway through by the end of next week." I find myself saying to myself as I close up my iPad after another successful writing stint at a cafe.

If you are a musician, affirm that you will spend x minutes a day playing your instrument. You could be more strict with yourself and make sure you play those annoying scales or arpeggios. If you're a singer, you could resolve to do 15 minutes of scales every day. It's painful, not just for yourself and your neighbors, but, I assure you, these repetitive exercises really work.

These times that you set aside for creativity should be thought about seriously. There's no point in setting impossible or over-ambitious goals or routines. You know yourself better than anyone. So, no one can tell you what routine you should set yourself. But you should set yourself a goal that is both challenging and achievable.

## Embrace continuous learning

You can resolve to learn new skills. These new skills don't necessarily have to be in your primary discipline of choice. You can attend workshops, read books or study YouTube tutorials about an unrelated skill if it interests you.

For example, I was quite impressed and interested in some YouTube tutorials about playing the bass. I don't possess a bass guitar and I hadn't played one in decades. But, for some reason, I became quite interested in the bass. I started to listen to the bassist instead of listening to the guitarist when I went to see bands. I became incredibly impressed by some extra talented bassists and appreciated more what the bassist brings to the overall sound, whereas in the past, I'd been quite dismissive. And, then coincidentally, I suddenly had the opportunity to play the bass in a bar every week with some really great musicians. I was able to jump in and not completely embarrass myself in comparison to the other guys I was playing with. And, now, playing the bass is giving me some extra understanding on playing my main instrument, the guitar. It's given me insights into one of my most elusive and highly sought after goals, playing solos. I have always sucked at playing guitar solos and I've always wanted to be able to wow audiences with a kickass solo. Well, this skill is, sadly, still a long way off. But, I'm getting there. And playing the bass, something I previously wouldn't have been interested in, has helped me play guitar better. It's the continuous improvement of a skill set that is one of the pleasures of creativity. You get better and better.

You'll never know where the creative journey or the learning journey will take you. So, read books about subjects you are not usually interested in. Watch movies in genres you don't know much about. Attend workshops for skills you don't currently have. All creative disciplines are connected. It's not initially obvious where they are connected. Join the dots, marry different ideas together, and explore different neural pathways in your mind. This is what creativity is all about.

## Seek feedback

We have already discussed the importance of a support network or a group of likeminded people who will encourage you. You can use this group for feedback.

Whenever you start a new project or have any sort of project iteration finished, you should ask trusted individuals for feedback. This is a double-edged sword, of course. If you're just starting out, well-meaning criticism can be hard to take when you've put your heart into your work. But, if you trust the individual concerned, feedback can be priceless especially if the individual is a likely consumer of your work.

However, as you move along the creative path, and have a few "successes" or achievements under your belt, you'll develop a thicker skin. Then you'll be able to offer up ideas or iterations of your art to the general public on social media. If you are a photographer, artist, musician or writer, you could regularly post what you're up to online. It might be scary, but the feedback will be worth it. As a writer, I'm telling people online that I'm writing a book on creativity and asking people for ideas. I can guarantee someone somewhere will say something that I'll find interesting and include in the final manuscript.

It might be scary. But embarking on a creative venture without external feedback is destined for failure. You'll be constantly second-guessing people's reactions to you. You'll question yourself and suffer imposter syndrome. Seek feedback early and regularly.

## Self evaluate

Not only should you be continually seeking feedback from others, you should be seeking feedback from yourself. This can be a part of your creative journal.

Identify your strengths and weaknesses. Think of ways you can improve your weaknesses and think of ways you can create more art that shows your strengths. Set goals and deadlines for when you should be able to master a particular skill in a particular creative discipline. You may miss the deadline but that wouldn't be the end of the world. Self evaluation isn't self criticism. However, it will mean you have a path with milestones in your creative journal.

## Be kind to yourself

Your happiness is of paramount importance to you. Without your happiness, you can't make anyone else happy. Prioritizing self-care will help ignite and nurture your creativity. Take care of your physical and mental well-being. Get enough sleep, eat a balanced diet, exercise regularly, and manage stress levels.

You may think Van Gogh living on a diet of cigarettes and coffee or Keith Richards's excesses helped them on their creative path. But, the opposite is more likely. The creative energy was there despite the hard lives they led, not because of them.

Self-care involves watching what you put into your body, both physically and mentally. We all know that eating a load of fatty foods as well as drinking excess alcohol is bad for us. Fatty foods produce cholesterol that clogs up arteries increasing the risk of a heart attack. Alcohol is a poison and too much of it also worsens our health.

However, we spend less time worrying about the thoughts we put in our heads than what substances we put in our bodies. And our mental health is just as important. This is why I think it's extremely important to regulate what media we consume. We live in a world where humans of all ages regularly flick through social media timelines which sophisticated artificial intelligence have designed specifically to make us angry and afraid. Personally, I think timelines are evil and I've recently expelled them from my life altogether.

Maybe you won't agree with me and don't want to sound preachy. After all, it's totally up to you what media you consume. All I can say is it's improved my mental condition.

Now, I never look at a timeline which curates content for me. I go out and search for content I want to consume. If I want to know how to play something on the guitar, I'll search for it on YouTube. I have deleted Facebook from my phone and I only use Messenger.

The result is I'm always the last to know something important (births, deaths, marriages). But, if it's important, I'll find out the old-fashioned way, usually by good old word of mouth. I'm lucky that I'm in my mid fifties so Instagram, TikTok, etc., don't interest me. I did have an annoying Twitter habit which, I'm delighted to say, I have stopped. I'll occasionally post on Twitter, LinkedIn, and Facebook and respond to notifications, but I never look at a timeline. I've learned my lesson.

What have I replaced it with? Creativity. The devil finds work for idle hands. I have noticed that retired people or people with little to engage themselves with are particularly prone to social media induced anger and fear. This is one of the reasons I consider creativity important. It keeps me engaged with people and actively pursuing something. It gives me a sense of purpose and meaning. A life without meaning means no reason for living. I think there is a connection between the rise in social media use and the rise in suicides.

Back to self-care. Yes, physical health is important. We should engage ourselves in some sort of regular exercise like running or swimming. We should watch what we eat, drink and not smoke cigarettes (and not too much of anything else). But we should also watch what we think. And watch what we say.

I want you to think of people you know who are happy. And I want you to think of people who you consider to be unhappy. How do they compare when you meet them? The unhappy people will be negative, complaining and will be regularly putting people down. And the happy people you know will be positive, won't be complaining, and will be regularly encouraging and praising others.

This is also true in the creative world. Some of the most happy and successful musicians have praised me and encouraged me. And, by the same token, negative, unhappy people tend to criticize other musicians in order to feel better about themselves. I'm sure you've noticed this before. I can remember the occasions when a really good musician has praised me or thanked me for my input. It made me feel ten feet tall. Praise and thanks go a long way.

So, in the course of your life, give genuine thanks and praise. It's difficult if you're not used to it but it becomes easier with time. Be positive about the art you love. Constantly encourage and praise those artists and people you admire. The purpose of art is to elevate the human condition. So elevate those that are elevating others. If you are positive and encouraging to people you admire online and in real life, you will draw these people to you. You will feed off their positivity and creativity, inspiring a virtuous circle of creative energy.

We are indulging in creativity to make ourselves feel better and be happy. Try to make yourself happier for creativity, as well. Engaging in self-care practices ensures you have the physical energy and mental clarity to make yourself a better artist and a better person.

## Mindfulness and meditation

Mindfulness and meditation greatly benefits the creative process as it promotes a deeper connection to the present moment, enhances focus, and reduces mental clutter.

Meditation is non-judgmental present moment awareness. We have discussed the process of meditation earlier in this book. It very often involves sitting quietly and concentrating on the present moment, usually by concentrating on your breathing.

Mindfulness is almost the same thing but it is generally concentrating on the present moment whilst you're doing something else. Buddhist monks aim to spend their monastic life in total mindfulness. Whether they are eating, studying, walking or meditating, they aim to always be in the moment.

Mindfulness is allied with creativity because the total absorption in the creative process can produce a "flow state" where the past and future disappears and you are totally in the moment.

## Keep a creative journal

Journaling your creative endeavors is an extremely productive way to make sure you stick to your creative journey.

As I've said elsewhere in this book, I have been journaling every day for over two years now. It's not only improved my writing but it's also allowed me to transport my thoughts onto digital paper so that they don't stew in my head. I put down all my creative highlights, thoughts, and goals in the journal as well.

I will record in my journal about my performances in bars in town. I'll say what songs went down well. What I enjoyed about certain venues. And which musicians I enjoyed playing with. I will also talk about my business. I'll mention if I'd had a particularly good session writing a section of this book in which cafe. I'll also talk about challenges in my business, how I'd failed to get a particular AI model to work on my computer, for example.

These are all important facts that I can refer back to in future years. I forget which songs where I've played them sometimes and my journal can remind me of successes I've had in the past that I would have otherwise forgotten.

But you can be even more detailed in a dedicated creative journal. You can journal about your creative journey and nothing else. So, whether you wanted to write a book, exhibit your work, or air some sort of performance, you could specify all the milestones and goals you wanted to achieve. Then you could journal about all the steps you'll need to take to achieve your creative endeavor. And then, whether you achieve your goals by the deadline or not, you will learn so much about yourself and your creative processes through the practice of journaling.

## Actionable takeaways

**Set Aside Time for Creativity**: Dedicate specific time for your creative pursuits. This could be writing a certain number of words each day, or spending a set amount of time playing an instrument. Make these goals challenging but achievable.

**Embrace Continuous Learning**: Always be open to learning new skills, even if they're not directly related to your primary creative discipline. Attend workshops, read books, or watch tutorials on a variety of subjects. This can lead to unexpected insights and enhance your overall creativity.

**Seek Feedback**: Regularly seek feedback from trusted individuals or a support network. This can provide valuable insights and help you improve your work. Be open to criticism and use it constructively to improve your craft.

**Self-Evaluate**: Regularly evaluate your strengths and weaknesses. Set goals for improving your weaknesses and enhancing your strengths. Use a creative journal to track your progress and set milestones.

**Be Kind to Yourself**: Prioritize self-care. Your physical and mental well-being are crucial for maintaining creativity. Get enough sleep, eat a balanced diet, exercise regularly, and manage stress levels. Above all, meditate regularly and practice gratitude.

**Keep a Creative Journal**: Document your creative journey in a dedicated journal. This can help you track your progress, set goals, and reflect on your creative process.

Remember, maintaining a creative lifestyle is a journey, not a destination. Be patient with yourself and enjoy the process.

# Grandma Moses

Anna Mary Robertson Moses, known as Grandma Moses, was born on September 7, 1860, in Greenwich, New York. Moses lived a life deeply connected to the rural landscapes that would later become the subjects of her acclaimed paintings.

Before her late 70s, Moses led a life centered around family and farm work. She married Thomas Salmon Moses in 1887 and raised ten children while managing the daily demands of a working farm. Although her artistic inclinations were evident in her embroidery and needlework, it wasn't until her later years that she discovered a passion for painting.

In the late 1930s, at the age of 78, Moses faced physical limitations preventing her from continuing with embroidery. As a result, she turned to painting as a new creative outlet. Inspired by landscapes of her childhood, Moses began capturing scenes of rural life with a fresh perspective.

Using simple materials like house paint and old pieces of wood or cardboard, Grandma Moses brought to life the beauty of the countryside. Her paintings often depicted farm activities, landscapes, and scenes from daily life, resonating with viewers who were captivated by her unique style and nostalgic themes.

Moses's work gained attention when an art collector, Louis J. Caldor, discovered her paintings in a local drugstore window. He recognized the extraordinary talent in her artwork and arranged for her first solo exhibition in New York City in 1940. The exhibition was a resounding success.

From that point forward, Grandma Moses's career blossomed. She became a celebrated artist, exhibiting her work across the United States and internationally. Her paintings, characterized by their folk art charm and warm depictions of rural life, struck a chord with audiences of all ages and backgrounds.

Grandma Moses continued to paint prolifically until her passing at the age of 101 in 1961. Her story reminds us that it's never too late to follow our passions, explore our creative talents, and bring beauty into the world.

# Step six: How to share yourself creatively

It's important not to keep all your art to yourself. There comes a point where you have to share your creative work. You owe it to the world.

Every artist creates art for themselves. True artists don't do it for ego. However, this doesn't mean creativity exists in a vacuum. The very action of sharing your creativity is creative.

Sharing yourself creatively helps you see value in what you do. It will boost your confidence and encourage you to create more and more and then to share more and more.

By sharing, you will inspire others and create a community of like-minded creatives that follow your lead.

## Overcoming the fear of judgment

"Feel the fear and do it anyway". It's easy to say. I have written 8 books, performed my songs in front of hundreds of strangers and regularly email my work to thousands of people. And my flimsy male ego still gets hurt and feels shame on a regular basis. Maybe I'm not the best person to give advice on this matter.

You have to embrace vulnerability even if other people don't. You will feel fear. We all do. It's part of being human. Just remember, it will pass, eventually.

Remind yourself why you started all this. You started to be creative because there is something inside you that you value. You picked up this book because you recognized something inside you that you want to express.

Every creative has a burning need to share. They wouldn't be creatives otherwise. It's an essential part of why you are creative.

## Receiving feedback gracefully

There's definitely a right way and a wrong way to give feedback. But, people who leave one star reviews on Amazon about a book that you put your heart into, probably aren't aware of that.

However, you should always try to understand the negative feedback, even if you don't completely take it on board. You've got to believe in yourself, after all. But feedback should always be listened to respectfully when at all possible. You might not understand fully where the person is coming from but you can try to understand it from their perspective. You can try to ask clarifying questions if you really don't understand.

At the end of the day, you should always seek to understand your audience. Those who support you are great. But those who criticize you are also your audience. What was it that brought them to your creation in the first place?

Negative feedback is more useful than praise, so don't block it out.

## Sharing your work online

We have already discussed various ways to share online. Seek out various communities and hashtags by identifying creative work that you identify with and post in these places.

Post regularly.

Online sharing and creating a community is an ongoing process. If you haven't started, start now. If you haven't started posting, then you don't have a following. So there's no point worrying about your first post. No one's going to see it, so post it!

This is the frustrating part of social media sharing. You really have to keep at it. And it can be soul destroying at first. But you can encourage friends and family to look at your first offerings. This way, you will get some encouragement to start the ball rolling.

I've been sharing digital art that I've created using Midjourney and enhancing in Adobe Photoshop recently. These posts get some "Likes" and traction. It's important not to compare yourself with those posts that seem to get thousands of comments in a few minutes.

You may like to shop around when it comes to finding communities.

Present your creations in the best possible manner. Give background to the creative process when necessary. Be honest. Tailor your posts to the platform and the audience.

You can also post updates about your work. Even post your work in progress. Share some tips about techniques you are using. All the above can make you vulnerable. But this is the most important point. Creativity teaches us to be OK with vulnerability.

## Teaching online, starting a website and an email list

You can take online sharing to a completely new level after a while, if you wish. Once you become more confident in your creative skills, you can share more and more about the techniques you use to create your art. You will have been doing it for a while by this point. And, if so, people will want to know more about how you get things done.

If you do want to share your creative progress, there are online learning platforms that sell video courses, like Udemy. These platforms can be great for growing an audience.

As your audience becomes bigger and bigger, you may like to take things to the next stage and start a website and an email list. This will take more time to accomplish and will incur a monthly cost but, if done successfully, it will be worth it. An email list of hardcore fans will give you leverage online as you can direct this faithful group of people to your latest online offerings. This will give all your future work an initial boost.

## Sharing your creativity offline

The best way to share your material will be "face to face" with your audience in the real world. This may be difficult for individuals who don't live in large cities and in places where there aren't facilities for artistic interaction. I've researched organizations to help you in this book already. They are in the "Step four: Unleash Creativity"" section.

## Actionable takeaways

**Share Your Work**: Don't keep your creative work to yourself. Sharing your creativity can help you see value in what you do, boost your confidence, and inspire others.

**Overcome the Fear of Judgment**: Embrace vulnerability and know that fear is a part of the creative process. Remember why you started your creative journey and use that as motivation to share your work.

**Receive Feedback Gracefully**: Listen to feedback respectfully, even if it's negative. Try to understand it from the giver's perspective and use it to improve your work.

**Share Your Work Online**: Regularly post your work on various online platforms. Tailor your posts to the platform and audience, and consider sharing work-in-progress updates and technique tips.

**Teach Online or Start a Website**: Once you're more confident in your skills, consider sharing more about your techniques through online learning platforms, starting a website, and creating an email list.

**Share Your Creativity Offline**: Engage with your audience in the real world. This could be through exhibitions, performances, or other face-to-face interactions.

**Understand Your Audience**: Both supporters and critics are part of your audience. Try to understand what brought them to your work and use this understanding to improve your creations.

Remember, sharing your creativity is a process. Be patient with yourself, and enjoy the journey of connecting with others through your creative work.

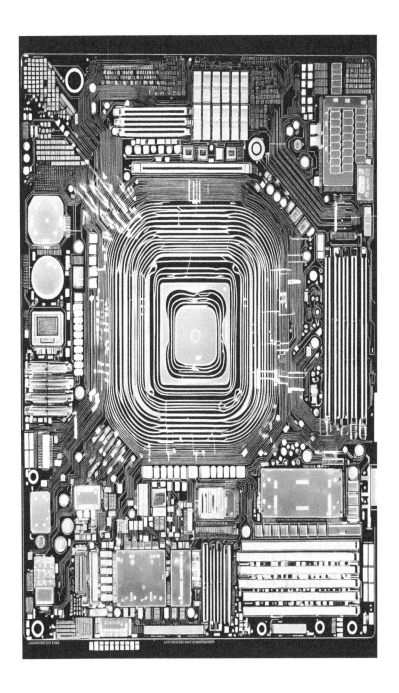

# The story of AlphaGo

In the world of Artificial Intelligence, a groundbreaking moment unfolded when Google DeepMind developed AlphaGo, an advanced program capable of playing the ancient game of Go at an unprecedented level. The story of AlphaGo's development and its challenge match against top Go player Lee Sedol in 2016 captivated the world.

The team at Google DeepMind sought to create an AI system that could master the complexities of Go, a game known for its immense complexity and strategic depth.

To truly assess AlphaGo's capabilities, the team sought out one of the world's top Go players, Lee Sedol, as their opponent in a five-game challenge match. Lee Sedol, a highly skilled player with multiple world titles to his name, was considered a formidable adversary for AlphaGo.

The match took place in March 2016 in Seoul, South Korea, and drew global attention. In a stunning display of AI prowess, AlphaGo won the first three games against Lee Sedol, showcasing its ability to navigate the complex Go board with strategic brilliance. The victory was not only a testament to the power of AI but also a moment of reflection for the world of Go, which had long been considered too intricate for a machine to master.

Despite facing a formidable opponent in AlphaGo, Lee Sedol showcased his remarkable resilience and adaptability. With the pressure mounting, he demonstrated incredible creativity and unconventional moves in the fourth game, securing a hard-fought victory. This unexpected outcome served as a reminder of the unique human capacity to innovate and think outside the box.

The match between AlphaGo and Lee Sedol marked a turning point in the field of AI and its impact on human creativity. The collaboration between AI and human expertise led to astonishing breakthroughs. Following the challenge match, it was reported that AlphaGo's unconventional moves and strategies profoundly influenced the Go community, including professionals and amateurs alike.

Korean Go players, in particular, were inspired by AlphaGo's playstyle and began experimenting with new approaches. One notable example was the Korean Go player Park Junghwan, who trained and played against AlphaGo on a regular basis. Park Junghwan's abilities and creativity saw considerable growth as he incorporated elements of AlphaGo's strategies into his own play.

The story of AlphaGo and its influence on Lee Sedol, Park Junghwan, and the Go playing community exemplifies how AI technologies can enhance human capabilities and spark new levels of creativity. It shows the symbiotic relationship between AI and human ingenuity, where machines augment human potential.

# Creativity and the future

The future is here already. The world is changing fast and we have to adapt to these changes. If you find the Global Financial Crisis, the pandemic, the war in Ukraine and climate change unsettling, I believe we're heading for more trauma as the world hurtles toward a future none of us can predict.

I'm speaking of advances in Artificial Intelligence, big data, biotechnology and other technological breakthroughs that will affect the global economy and our day-to-day lives.

Our jobs and careers will become more uncertain or even disappear completely with advances in computing and automation. If a computer or a robot can do your job more effectively, you can bet one day your boss will prefer a machine to you. This is one of the many reasons why I think human creativity is not only important but essential in our lives going forward.

## The need for creativity, critical thinking, and problem-solving

As AI and automation take over certain repetitive and routine tasks, I think we will have an extra need for creativity, critical thinking, and problem-solving. Creativity will become a distinguishing factor that sets individuals apart from machines.

Technological advancements will continually reshape

industries meaning joblessness and uncertainty. Those who embrace their creativity will be able to harness these technologies and work with them rather than against them. By thinking creatively, those that engage with it will identify novel applications for this new technology.

AI technologies excel at handling structured and predictable tasks, but they struggle to navigate complex and ambiguous situations. Those who cultivate their creativity can approach problems from multiple angles, and find innovative solutions by marrying two different AI approaches together or combining an AI solution with an offline human element.

Those who are facing unemployment may consider entrepreneurship. Creativity plays a crucial role in identifying market gaps and business ideas.

Ethical considerations will become increasingly important as AI technologies become more powerful and influential. Those with strong empathic qualities and knowledge of the technology can bring a humanistic perspective to AI. They will use their "humanness" to anticipate potential biases and understand their impact to ensure AI technologies align with ethical standards.

As with all new technologies, it will destroy some jobs and create others. It will create new roles that don't even exist at the moment. Roles such as UX/UI designers, innovation consultants, creative strategists, content creators, and data storytellers will change and be filled by those lucky enough to be at the forefront of this new paradigm. These careers will require a blend of creativity, technical knowledge, and the ability to problem-solve using this new technology.

But, it is not all about embracing creativity in the age of AI. It's also about using AI to enhance your creativity.

Creativity can be amplified by collaboration between humans and AI technologies. And I will give a few examples now.

## Creative writing with ChatGPT

ChatGPT has learned from a diverse range of text data from the Internet and is designed to generate human-like responses to prompts. ("Prompts" are the questions or the inputs you type into the chatbot). It doesn't really understand what you are typing in or what it spits out. It is not conscious. It's a statistical model trained to generate text based on patterns it has learned from data. But the data it has been trained on is massive, so huge that no individual human could process it. But this bot can. So its answers are sometimes impressive and human.

It can help someone with little writing experience who wishes to create a book, a story, or any written piece for the first time.

ChatGPT can brainstorm ideas and provide suggestions for topics. This is exactly how I used

ChatGPT to help me write this book. And I'm using ChatGPT to help me now. However, ChatGPT isn't writing this text. I am.

But, don't just ask the AI bot, "hey, give me a topic for a great story I can write?" That's too general. It's better if you narrow down the prompts somehow. So, what are you interested in? Do you particularly like Elizabethan romantic fiction? Ask it for some ideas of a love story between a lord and lady in Elizabethan times.

If you're stuck or experiencing writer's block, you can ask ChatGPT for ideas about what to write about next. The quality of the prompt is all important. The more information and context you put in, the better the ideas that will come back to you.

Once you have decided on an idea for your story, you can get the chatbot to come up with ideas for a storyline or content. Remember, these bots have been trained on huge amounts of data. They can recognize patterns in language and stories. They can recognize what's good and what's bad based on the feedback they get in the same way you can. But they've been trained on more data than you have. This is why they can be most helpful in the planning stage. They are likely to think of an idea you wouldn't have.

After the planning stage comes the research stage. If you need additional information or data to support your content, ChatGPT can offer suggestions on reliable sources. Remember to always check the "factual" information you get from ChatGPT. It sometimes just makes stuff up.

As you write, you can get ChatGPT to refine your content. You can input certain sections of your text and ask for suggestions on how to improve clarity or reorganize information to create a more coherent end product.

AI powered tools can assist in proofreading your work by identifying grammatical errors, offering sentence structure improvements, and suggesting alternative word choices. AI helps us already with the suggestions you get when you're texting. You may find these autocorrects as infuriating as I do sometimes but, if you are using this, you are already using AI to enhance or improve your writing style. You just didn't know it.

It can also provide feedback on overall writing style and tone. ChatGPT can provide writing tips to help improve your writing. You can ask for guidance on sentence structure, paragraph organization, effective introductions, and conclusions, making your content more engaging.

ChatGPT is a chatbot. It's essential to "chat" with it. Engaging in a conversation with ChatGPT allows you to write collaboratively. Anyone who's ever written a book will tell you that it's a sometimes lonely occupation. You can be desperate for any feedback or help at all. Yes, groups of humans are great to collaborate with.

But bouncing ideas off the model, discussing concepts, and refining content in real-time, is like sitting next to a super-knowledgeable friend or published author who will always steer you in the right direction.

Remember, it's essential to verify the suggestions ChatGPT provides. It's a powerful tool, but human judgment is still crucial. Having said that, I really do believe ChatGPT has made me a better writer and has made this book a better book.

## Music and technology

I'm writing this as a 55 year old with a specific interest in blues, jazz, and classic popular music that originated in the early twentieth century. I regularly play blues licks on my guitar that were popularized by Robert Johnson nearly 100 years ago. Robert Johnson didn't need YouTube, Spotify or performance enhancement. I do understand the reticence that musicians and others have with modern technology.

However, many years ago, technology improved so humans were able to produce better quality instruments. And now digital technology is revolutionizing the world of music.

Apps equipped with AI, like Yousician, can provide interactive tutorials, virtual lessons, and personalized practice plans for instrument learning. These tools can analyze your performance and offer tailored exercises to improve the areas where you are weakest.

AI can now write music. Music to me is about numbers. There are seven different notes in a scale. In any given key, a popular song usually starts on the root note chord, the 1st. The 4th and 5th major chords are the most often used. The 2nd and 7th are usually minors or 7 chords. The chorus usually starts on the 4th. The song will usually resolve back to the root note chord and so on. Music composition tools can identify patterns like these by analyzing thousands of songs. They can then generate new chord progressions, melodies, harmonies, and musical ideas. Technology can also help with lyrics. I have used online rhyming dictionaries to help me write song lyrics.

Again, the usual caveat, these tools serve only as creative assistants. They should not replace the human composer.

Once the song is composed and rehearsed, music production software will then assist in the recording. These tools offer a host of features such as autotuning, beat detection, and vast libraries of high-quality instrument sounds and samples.

Online platforms also facilitate remote music collaboration, allowing musicians from different locations to collaborate on projects in real-time. I have not yet tried this but there are many examples on YouTube of musicians from all over the world, who have never met in person, and have collaborated on a song.

For the music listener, streaming platforms and

recommendation systems powered by AI algorithms help users discover new music based on their preferences and listening history. These platforms can also expose musicians to a wider audience and provide valuable inspiration.

## Art and technology

Art is no different to music. Technology has had a significant impact on it. Starting with learning, online platforms can provide interactive tutorials, step-by-step guides, and virtual lessons for learning different artistic techniques.

Digital art has greatly benefited from AI and technology. Graphics tablets, digital drawing software, and painting apps provide artists with a range of digital tools and brushes that simulate traditional mediums. AI algorithms can also generate realistic textures, lighting effects, and assist in creating complex digital artworks.

3D modeling software and sculpting tools allow artists to create digital sculptures and 3D models. These tools enable precise manipulation of virtual objects, offer real-time rendering, and can be used for 3D printing or visual effects in film and animation.

AI-powered photo editing software provides advanced features like automatic retouching, object removal, and content-aware fill. In the past, you had to know how to use Photoshop to perform these edits. Now they can be perfectly performed for you with a prompt. These tools can help photographers enhance their photographs. And they can help artists composite images and experiment.

It goes without saying that AI and technology have transformed film and video production. Video editing software offers features like automated color grading, object tracking, and intelligent scene detection. Additionally, AI-powered visual effects tools provide realistic simulations, character animations, and virtual environments.

I often use AI image generators like Midjourney, Leonardo, and Stable Diffusion. You can prompt the model to create any image you desire to see. You can specify the subject of the image as well as the style. AI algorithms can analyze and mimic different artistic styles. You can even mix styles and objects together, generating never before seen creations. You can use these tools to apply the various styles to your own artworks, and create something unique. Again, when you instruct the AI model to give you an image of a dog, the AI model doesn't think in terms of "dog", it's been trained on millions of images and it just sees the values of the pixels, recognizes patterns, and then reproduces another version of a dog—sometimes with amazing results.

These images can then be put into online AI video apps to create movies. Soon ordinary people like you and me will be able to create cinema quality movies with amazing sound and image quality.

Just as with music, technology can enable remote artistic collaboration by providing shared platforms, cloud-based storage, and real-time feedback. Artists can collaborate on projects, share ideas, and work together irrespective of their physical locations.

And, also like in the music world, online platforms, social media, and recommendation systems help artists gain exposure and reach wider audiences. These platforms allow artists to showcase their work, connect with other artists, and virtually meet other artists for potential real-world collaborations.

## Technology and creativity

From using certain dyes and pigments to help early modern humans create art on cave walls to developing iron tools to craft better instruments, technology has helped improve our creative output for millennia.

Photography initially wasn't considered art. It was seen as a form of science. But from the 19th century to the present day, it's been a widely recognized art form.

I remember people telling me in the nineties that the introduction of desktop publishing was a bad thing because it enabled people without much experience to become graphic designers. Desktop publishing, in effect, democratized publishing and older designers who completed two- and three- year courses at art school weren't happy about it. Now we have online apps like

Canva making design even easier for the masses but the voices against such technologies have disappeared.

It is quite easy to make mistakes with AI. Sometimes, the computer misunderstands the prompt because the language used has been too vague. Imagine this mistake happening in a large industrial operation or in a nuclear plant.

However, ChatGPT, other AI chatbots, and AI image generators, assist the user based on the information the human gives the machine. While these tools offer suggestions and ideas, the creativity of the content ultimately lies with the user. ChatGPT is a tool that enhances the creative process but does not replace the individual's ability to be creative.

People who try to use this technology as an alternative to their creativity will quickly realize that they are doing it wrong. There have always been lazy people looking for a shortcut. But they soon get disappointed. Other people will see its benefit and use it constructively.

Yes, we must exercise caution when using AI tools. ChatGPT has been trained on the Internet. The Internet contains biases and inaccuracies so relying solely on AI-generated content means you are relying on potentially biased information. So it is important to check the information using your human intuition as I've said already.

The risks associated with AI are not inherent to ChatGPT itself but rather lie in how AI technologies are deployed.

ChatGPT can not replace human creativity. Creativity is a complex human expression. It comes from personal originality, imagination, and experience. AI models like ChatGPT do not possess true creative consciousness, emotion, or experience. They are based on patterns and statistical probabilities. You can see this when working with AI chatbots. After a while, their suggestions can be very cold, calculated, dry, prescriptive and workmanlike. That's because they're not human.

AI and technology are valuable creative allies. These advancements offer new possibilities, from assisting in learning artistic skills and providing tools for digital art, music composition, and poetry, to enabling collaboration and exposure.

## AI and other tech tools for creativity

**Collaborative music composition**: You can use AI-powered tools like Aiva https://www.aiva.ai/ or Ecrett Music https://ecrettmusic.com/ to create original music tracks.

**Virtual reality art**: If you're one of those people who likes to experience new worlds with a headset on, create virtual reality realms with tools like Tilt Brush https://www.tiltbrush.com/ or Google Blocks.

**Augmented reality storytelling**: Augmented reality (AR) enhances a real world setting whereas virtual reality (VR) is completely virtual (think, headsets and Apple's "ski mask"). You can create interactive narratives using augmented reality (AR) tools like ZapWorks https://zap.works/ or Unity's AR Foundation https://unity.com/, overlaying digital content onto the real world.

**AI-Generated visual art**: I do a lot of this. I have been involved in graphic design for well over three decades now, and I love messing around with images. AI-inspired Digital art and image generation has really taken off in 2023. Just think what art we'll be seeing in 2025?

There are a slew of online AI image generators that can produce images to a written prompt. My favorite is Midjourney https://www.midjourney.com. It's annoying that you have to use Discord to communicate with the image bot, but it is free for your first 25 images so you can see if you like it or not. Otherwise, I have also used Leonardo AI https://leonardo.ai/, DALL·E 2 https://openai.com/dall-e-2, and Stable Diffusion https://stablediffusionweb.com/ they all have their pros and cons. And there are more such as DeepArt. io ,RunwayML's StyleGAN https://app.runwayml.com/models/runway/StyleGAN, Deep Dream Generator https://deepdreamgenerator.com/, AIGreem https://

aigreem.com/ and Night Cafe Creator https://creator.nightcafe.studio/

These AI image generators only create images at a certain size. However, there are AI solutions for this. To make a 1000 by 1000 pixel image into a 3000 by 3000 pixel with little loss of quality, you can google "AI image upscaler". My favorite is Upscayl https://www.upscayl.org/ which runs on your computer and can do batch upscales.

I also regularly turn vector=style, cartoony or stylized images into vectors with https://vectorizer.ai/ or you can create vector artwork from scratch with https://www.recraft.ai/.

**Image editors**: So, you've used AI image generators to make your artwork, then upscaled them using AI, what's next? You can utilize AI-powered photo editing software like Adobe Photoshop https://www.adobe.com/ph_en/ or Luminar AI https://skylum.com/luminar to enhance and transform your art. Unfortunately, both of these applications have a subscription fee but there are alternatives. I personally love Affinity Photo https://affinity.serif.com/en-gb/photo/ which is a $70 one-off fee and the software is regularly updated. Totally free, however, is the open source GIMP https://www.gimp.org/

**Collaborative design with AI**: Once you have created your images with an AI image generator and enhanced them, you can then use free tools such as Canva https://www.canva.com/en_ph/ or Figma https://www.figma.com/ to design graphics, illustrations, or user interfaces.

**AI-driven writing prompts**: I have already written at length how you can use the AI chatbot ChatGPT to enhance your writing. You can also use writing assistants like Write With Transformer https://transformer.huggingface.co/ or AI Dungeon https://aidungeon.io/ to generate creative writing prompts and explore new ideas.

**AI-powered writing analysis**: Once you've used ChatGPT and other tools to get great ideas and enhance your writing style, you can then utilize tools like Grammarly https://www.grammarly.com/ or Hemingway Editor https://hemingwayapp.com/ to improve grammar and receive suggestions for further improvements.

There are other tools for creative writing feedback like ProWritingAid https://prowritingaid.com/ or Wordtune https://www.wordtune.com/ which improve clarity, grammar, and overall writing quality.

**AI-driven poetry generation**: Engage with AI poetry generators such as PoemPortraits https://

artsexperiments.withgoogle.com/poemportraits or Talk to Transformer https://app.inferkit.com/demo to inspire and co-create poetic expressions.

**Machine learning-assisted filmmaking**: You can use machine learning algorithms to analyze and enhance video.

**Interactive game design**: The creative discipline of video gaming can, of course, be enhanced by AI. You can explore game development platforms like Unity https://unity.com/ or Unreal Engine https://www.unrealengine.com/en-US to create immersive gaming experiences.

**Data visualization**: Utilize data visualization tools like Tableau https://www.tableau.com/ or Datawrapper https://www.datawrapper.de/ to transform complex data sets into visually appealing and informative graphics, aiding in storytelling and communication.

**AI-enhanced fashion design**: You can leverage AI fashion assistants like Vue.ai https://vue.ai/ or Artifi Labs https://www.artifilabs.com/ to help with the fashion design process.

**AI-driven animation**: You can experiment with animation software like Adobe Character Animator https://www.adobe.com/ph_en/products/character-animator.html or Toon Boom Harmony https://www.toonboom.com/products/harmony, which incorporate AI features to automate character movement or lip-syncing.

**AI-generated concept art**: You can use AI art platforms like ArtBreeder https://www.artbreeder.com/ or DeepDream Generator https://deepdreamgenerator.com/ and generate unique and imaginative concept art.

**Music production**: There are AI-powered music production tools like LANDR https://www.landr.com/ or AI Mastering https://aimastering.com/ that you can use to enhance audio tracks.

**AI-driven storyboarding**: Plotagon https://www.plotagon.com/desktop/ and Storyboard AI https://krock.io/storyboard-ai/ visualize storytelling elements for film, animation, or any interactive narrative you wish.

**AI-enhanced choreography**: AI tools like Radical https://radicalmotion.com/ or DeepMotion Avatar https://www.deepmotion.com/ can help you to explore new movements and experiment with virtual dancers.

# The future of creativity

As we tackle the fast-paced challenges of this crazy world, I believe that creativity is not a luxury, but an essential skill. With the rise of Artificial Intelligence, big data, biotechnology, and automation, our working lives will become more uncertain. In this landscape, creativity, critical thinking, and problem-solving stand as distinguishing factors that set us apart from machines.

In this age of AI, we're not just embracing creativity, we're using AI to enhance it, no matter what creative discipline.

However, as we leverage these technologies, we must also be mindful of the risks and ethical considerations. AI is a powerful tool, but it's not without its challenges. It's essential to exercise caution, verify the information, and always check it with our human intuition.

Remember, creativity is a complex human expression that comes from our personal imagination and our personal experiences. AI models, while powerful, do not possess true creative consciousness, emotion, or experience. They are based on patterns and statistical probabilities. Use them as tools to enhance your creativity, not replace it. As we step into the future, let's carry our creativity with us, using it as our compass in this ever-evolving landscape.

# Enhancing creativity: A Final Note

As we draw the curtain on my little book on creativity, let's take a moment to acknowledge YOU. You are not a blank canvas but a rich tapestry of life experiences, memories, skills, and insights. Your creativity is your history, mingled with your dreams, and amplified by your curiosity.

## The wonders of perpetual learning

We have emphasized throughout this book the transformative power of learning. Not merely acquiring new skills or information but also nurturing an attitude of curiosity and openness. Perpetual learning enhances your creative and mental abilities and enriches your life.

## Cultivating creativity

Remember, creativity is not a finite resource but something that flourishes the more it is used. The seeds of new ideas need to be nurtured with patience, persistence, and positivity. Overcoming creative blocks, cultivating healthy habits, exploring new horizons, and embracing mistakes as stepping stones to success are the cornerstones of this creative garden.

## Riding the waves of change

In our rapidly evolving world, change is the only constant. Your creative potential will depend on your ability to ride the waves of change. The tools and strategies explored in this book are your compass in this voyage.

## Embracing connection

Creativity doesn't exist in isolation. It thrives in the connections we make—with people, ideas, and the world around us. Engaging in creative collaborations and building on the ideas of others will enrich your own creative output.

As we conclude our journey, it's important to remember that creativity is not a destination but a path of discovery, a journey of growth, and a dance of the mind. While the road may sometimes seem challenging, the destination is invariably rewarding.

Stay curious. Stay creative. Keep expanding your horizons and challenging the status quo. There is no end to this journey; there's only the thrill of what comes next, the joy of creating, the magic of turning ideas into reality. Carry these lessons with you and, in doing so, shape the world with the power of your creativity.